Lobbying Illinois

How You Can Make a Difference in Public Policy

by
Christopher Z. Mooney
and
Barbara Van Dyke-Brown

Institute
for
Legislative
Studies

Abraham Lincoln Presidential · Center for Governmental Studies

UIS
UNIVERSITY
of ILLINOIS at
SPRINGFIELD
SPRINGFIELD, ILLINOIS

ISBN: 0-938943-22-7

With permission, portions of this book are revised and updated from the *Manual of Public Interest Lobbying* published in 1978 and 1984 by the Illinois State Support Center and *Lobbying for the Public Schools* published by the Illinois Association of School Boards in 1985 and 1990.

Text and cover design: Diana L.C. Nelson
Printer: Phillips Brothers Printers

Printed in the United States of America
Second Printing - 2003

10 9 8 7 6 5 4 3 2 1

Institute for Legislative Studies, PAC 466
University of Illinois at Springfield
One University Plaza, MS PAC 466
Springfield, IL 62703-5407

Phone: (217) 206-6574
Fax: (217) 206-6542
E-mail: ils@uis.edu
Web site: http://ils.uis.edu

This book is dedicated to
all the citizens of Illinois who dare to
make a difference in the policy-making
process, and to the lobbyists, legislative
staff, and legislators who have generously
shared their knowledge and expertise
with us over the years. And it is especially
dedicated to our favorite Illinoisans —
Laura, Allison, Charlie, Randy, and Justin.

Table of Contents

Preface

We wrote this book in the spirit that all citizens deserve to have their opinions heard and their interests considered in the policy-making process. We believe that representative government works best when citizens have a clear public voice and take an active interest in politics and government. Too many people think of government as an entity that is *out there* and does things *to* or *for* us. Government ought to be *of us*, a tool that the people use to do collectively what they cannot do alone. The more people work together with other like-minded people to advocate their common interests in the policy-making process, the more government will reflect the will and values of the people of Illinois.

All proceeds from the sale of this book will help fund the civic and educational activities of Institute for Legislative Studies at the University of Illinois at Springfield. Our mission is:

- to generate and disseminate information about the Illinois General Assembly, U.S. state legislatures, and U.S. state public policy;
- to promote public interest in and understanding of the legislative process in Illinois, other states, and at the national level;
- to enhance the quality of the legislative process in Illinois; and
- to promote the academic study of state legislatures and state politics.

As you are reading and using this book, keep in mind that the law and the legislative process are fluid. There will always be changes in specific rules and requirements, and especially in telephone numbers, Web site addresses, and so forth. But in reviewing this information, we believe that you will find that the basic principles of effective lobbying remain constant. Indeed, these principles are likely to be just as applicable to your lobbying efforts in 2013 as in 2003, and just as effective in lobbying other state governments, the United States Congress, or a local school board as they are in lobbying the Illinois General Assembly. We trust that following these principles will help you to become a more effective advocate for your group.

Acknowledgments

Many people had a role in bringing this project to fruition. First, some parts of this book began in the *Manual of Public Interest Lobbying* published by the Illinois State Support Center in 1978 and 1984 and in *Lobbying for Public Schools* published by the Illinois Association of School Boards in 1985 and 1990. We have significantly revised, updated, and expanded the excerpts we used from these publications. We wish to acknowledge the work of the many advocates and writers who worked on these earlier projects for their great service to the citizens of Illinois and to this book. Second, many current and former lobbyists and others involved in the Illinois legislative process reviewed all or parts of this book in manuscript form and offered many important suggestions and ideas: Dan Burkhalter, Illinois Education Association; James R. Covington, III, Illinois State Bar Association; Claire B. Eberle, Joint Committee on Administrative Rules; Richard C. Edwards, Legislative Reference Bureau; Scott Humbard, Chemical Industry Council of Illinois; David A. Joens, Office of the Illinois Secretary of State; Rebecca W. Owens, formerly with the United Way of Illinois; Donald J. Payton, Illinois State Board of Education; James Russell, Illinois Association of School Boards; Ben Schwarm, Illinois Association of School Boards; Steve Stalcup, Office of the Illinois Secretary of State; and Vicki Thomas, Joint Committee on Administrative Rules. Third, several UIS staff helped immensely with the production of this book: Brad Bonnette, Lorrie Farrington, Jon Francois, Karen Kunz, Rodd Whelpley, and Ed Wojcicki. We offer special thanks to Diana Nelson for her excellent design work on the cover and throughout the book. Finally, we would like to thank the staff photographers of the four legislative caucuses for their generosity in allowing us to use their work: Jay Barnard (Senate Republicans), Kelvin Kelso (House Republicans), Jessica Kolb (Senate Democrats), and Russ Nagel (House Democrats).

Regardless of all the assistance we have received in writing this book, we accept full responsibility for any errors or omissions.

Illustration Credits

Our thanks to all those who contributed art, photography, and document examples to *Lobbying Illinois*.

Cover photo by Diana L.C. Nelson

Chapter 1

Chapter 2

Chapter 3

Chapter 4

Chapter 5

Chapter 6

Chapter 7

Chapter 8

Chapter 9

Chapter **1**
The Importance of Lobbying

L obbying is the systematic effort to affect public policy by influencing the views of policy-makers whether in a state legislature, city council, government agency, or anywhere else decisions are made that affect citizens and businesses. Over the years, the term "lobbying" has acquired a negative connotation. But lobbying is nothing more than the organized and intensive exercise of a citizen's constitutional right to petition the government. In fact, lobbying makes an important contribution to effective and responsive government by making vital information available to public officials who cannot possibly know the full impact of every law and regulation that comes before them.

To be effective, lobbyists need to make a certain point of view interesting and relevant to policy-makers. They must select the right arguments, perspectives, strategies, and activities and present them in a way that grabs the attention of decision-makers. The lobbyist, in effect, makes a place at the table for the concerns of the group represented.

Lobbyists work to influence policy-making in many ways, including:

- Ensuring that the voices of those they represent are heard by policy-makers;

- Providing technical information and advice to policy-makers, the news media, and citizens;
- Pulling together opposing interests to negotiate compromise;
- Acting as catalysts to keep policy-makers, allied groups, and the media excited about the issues of concern to their clients.

This book focuses on legislative lobbying, particularly in the Illinois General Assembly. Legislative lobbying takes many forms. It can be in the public domain or behind the scenes. It can be as mundane as presenting highly technical information or as lofty as laying out a group's basic moral values. It can aim to set up a new program, change an existing one, guarantee certain rights, secure funding, or alter the decision of a government agency. While the targets, goals, and tactics of lobbying vary with each situation, applying the principles of effective lobbying maximizes the impact of your group's views at all levels and in all types of legislative and government decision-making.

Citizen Lobbying

The First Amendment to the United States Constitution guarantees the right of citizens to petition the government—

Lobbying: The systematic effort to affect public policy by influencing the views of policy-makers.

❝Congress shall make no law...abridging... the right of the people peaceably to assemble, and to petition the government for a redress of grievances.❞

—Amendment 1, U.S. Constitution

that is, to communicate their views to legislative bodies and administrative agencies. In addition, the Illinois Constitution guarantees Illinois citizens the right "to make known their opinions to their representatives and to apply for redress of grievances" (Article I, Section 5). Many Americans choose to make their opinions known to government by working together in groups with like-minded citizens and, often, by hiring specialists—lobbyists—to present those views.

Lobbyists play an important role in public policy-making. They provide policy-makers with information about policy impacts and options and about citizens' opinions. They help develop dialogue and compromise among groups that may be at odds with one another. Lobbyists even facilitate interactions among policy-makers themselves, allowing for more efficient and effective government.

The basic premise of this book is that lobbying, carried out and supported by individual citizens and groups, is a critical component of the policy-making process. For a representative democracy to work properly, citizens have the right—and indeed, the obligation—to make themselves heard.

Unfortunately, lobbying has the reputation of leaning toward the seamy side of politics, where bribery and threats are the tools, and corruption is the result. Indeed, there was a period in history when such an image may have been all too accurate in Illinois and elsewhere. But today, despite a few well-publicized

exceptions, the vast majority of legislators and lobbyists are decent, honest, dedicated people who have the best interests of the state—or at least the best interests of their constituents—at heart. A changed public ethos, more vigilant journalists, a more educated public, and increased government regulation have largely cleaned up politics, and lobbying, in Illinois and across the nation.

Many grassroots organizations and community groups mistakenly believe that money and political intimidation are required to have an impact on public policy and that only the rich and powerful have that kind of influence. But it is crucial to remember that *all* legislators— on the federal, state, and local levels—are politicians whose continued success depends on their ability to satisfy voting constituents. Re-election, recognition, and status are powerful motivators. Effective lobbying can wield as much influence on these outcomes as the biggest corporation or trade association.

How This Book Can Help

Lobbying is an integral part of civic life. An organization that does not lobby, or does not lobby effectively, will be less likely to have its interests reflected in public policy than an organization that does lobby effectively. Make no mistake about it—hundreds of organizations work every day to influence policy-makers at all levels of government. To make a difference in the content and implementation of public policy, lobbying is essential.

This book will help you learn to lobby effectively and maximize your chances for success in the policy-making arena. In Chapters 2-4, you will learn the basics of lobbying Illinois state government. Chapter 2 gives a brief outline of the Illinois state legislative process. Chapter 3 provides some

Constitution of the State of Illinois is the organizational document that establishes the general laws and principles of government for the State of Illinois. Copies of this document may be found in numerous sources, including: the *Illinois Blue Book*, *Handbook of Illinois Government*, and the Illinois General Assembly Web site (http://www.legis.state.il.us/). Copies of the *Illinois Blue Book* and the *Handbook of Illinois Government* are available free of charge from the Illinois Secretary of State's office – (217) 782-5763.

important dos and don'ts of lobbying and the basic tools of the trade. Chapter 4 contains a more detailed discussion of the rules and procedures of the legislative process and discusses how these can be used to aid the lobbying effort. Chapter 5 provides information for the more experienced lobbyist on a variety of strategies and tactics. Chapters 6-8 discuss specific aspects of lobbying that are useful for developing experience and expertise. Chapter 6 covers an increasingly important topic: how to lobby state agencies and work through the administrative rules process. Chapter 7 covers grassroots politics and outlines ways to energize and organize groups for political action. Chapter 8 discusses lobbying regulations and ethics—vital information for every lobbyist and group. Throughout the book, numerous examples of documents necessary for success as a lobbyist are also highlighted. Finally, Chapter 9 lists a wide range of resources vital to your lobbying efforts. ❑

"Any group that can be touched by state government cannot afford to be without representation. If groups do not realize the need for a lobbyist at the outset, they soon learn their lesson. For example, Florida's cities appealed to the legislature for the enactment of a program that would have facilitated urban development. The legislature was willing to accede but insisted that the cities come up with a revenue source to fund the program they wanted. Everyone searched for a source. They found it in the dry-cleaning business, one of the only groups without a lobbyist in Tallahassee. With no one in the legislature speaking against it, a sales tax was imposed on dry cleaning. Within a few days of the tax's enactment, the dry cleaners had gotten themselves a lobbyist."

—Alan Rosenthal (1993, 5)

The Illinois Statehouse.

Chapter 2

A Primer on the Illinois Legislative Process

The process that moves a policy from an idea to law in Illinois is arcane and complex. This is no accident. The legislative process is designed to be complicated and difficult for a number of reasons. Americans are suspicious of government and view it as a threat to personal liberty. As a result, our political institutions are set up to limit government power as much as possible. Furthermore, the passage of a law is a significant event that can have major implications for people and business in the state. If the state is going to ban, mandate, or tax something, considerable thought must be given to doing so. Finally, given the variety of interests and values of the citizens of Illinois, the process must provide many opportunities for people to express their opinions and be assured that their concerns are heard. In other words, the legislative process is complicated and difficult in order to protect Illinoisans.

The legislative process can be thought of as an intricate labyrinth. A bill generally clears one obstacle after another in a fairly

Fact:

In the 91st Illinois General Assembly (1999-2000), 6,748 bills were introduced, but only 954 (14%) became law.

The floor of the Illinois House of Representatives.

specific and routine order as it moves toward becoming law. Failure to pass any of these obstacles successfully can stop a bill's progress. Thus, it is much easier to prevent a bill from becoming law than it is to see one successfully through to final passage. Each of the obstacles is, in fact, a test of the quality of the bill. Most bills will not survive one of these tests and will fall by the wayside. For example, in the 91st Illinois General Assembly (1999-2000), 6,748 bills were introduced, but only 954 (14 percent) became law. However, bills that represent worthy ideas, that resonate with legislators and other interested people surrounding the process, not only have a better chance of passing these tests, they will develop and improve because of them.

The Illinois Constitution and the internal rules of each chamber of the General Assembly define the legislative path and its obstacles. These rules are passed at the beginning of each two-year cycle of the General Assembly in January of odd-numbered years. Under certain circumstances, the rules may be suspended or even changed by vote of the chamber. While these shortcuts do exist for important, unusual, or emergency bills, don't depend on these shortcuts working to your advantage. It is far more important to know all the aspects of the normal legislative process and to stay within its confines. Consider any shortcuts that you receive in the process a rare bonus.

The lobbyist's main job is to guide favored bills along to passage and to prevent passage of bills the client opposes. In this chapter, we provide a brief description of the major features and players in the process.

General Assembly Workloads, 1991-2000

	87ND 1991-92	88TH 1993-94	89TH 1995-96	90TH 1997-98	91ST* 1999-2000
Bills introduced	6,505	6,128	5,734	5,863	6,678
Sent to governor	1,528	775	746	887	990
% of bills introduced	23.5%	12.6%	13.0%	15.1%	14.8%
Approved by governor	1,264	671	679	830	925
% of bills sent to governor	82.7%	86.6%	91.0%	93.6%	93.4%
Reduction or item-vetoed	26	0	0	0	0
% of bills sent to governor	1.7%	0.0%	0.0%	0.0%	0.0%
Veto of entire bill	174	54	21	68	53
% of bills sent to governor	11.4%	7.0%	2.9%	7.7%	5.4%
Overridden	14	4	2	16	6
% of vetoes	8.0%	7.4%	9.5%	23.5%	11.3%
Amendatorily vetoed	90	50	46	53	40
% of bills sent to governor	5.9%	6.5%	6.2%	6.0%	4.0%
Accepted	64	16	36	32	22
% of vetoes	71.1%	32.0%	78.3%	60.4%	55.0%
Overridden	2	1	1	2	0
% of vetoes	2.2%	2.0%	2.2%	3.8%	0.0%
No action (died)	21	33	9	16	12
% of vetoes	23.3%	66.0%	19.6%	30.2%	30.0%
Laws enacted	1,280	692	718	819	925
% of bills introduced	19.7%	11.3%	12.5%	14.0%	13.9%
% of bills sent to governor	83.8%	89.3%	92.2%	92.3%	93.4%

*Data for 91st General Assembly as of August 7, 2000.
SOURCE: Adapted from Legislative Research Unit, *Preface to Lawmaking*, November 2000, p.2.11.

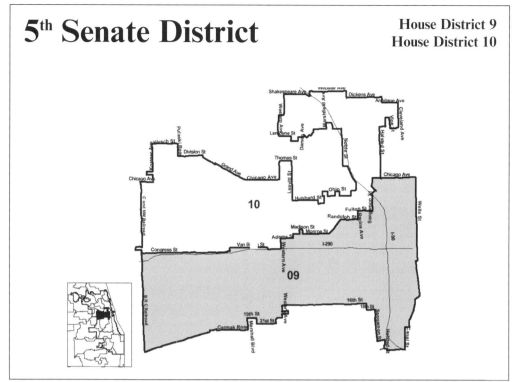

5th Senate District

Bicameral: The Illinois state legislature is bicameral because it has two legislative chambers—a Senate and a House of Representatives. The U.S. Congress and 49 U.S. state legislatures are bicameral. Only Nebraska has a unicameral legislature (known as "The Unicam"), having a Senate but no House.

This is the map of the 5th State Senate district for the elections of 2002-2010. A senator from this district would probably focus his or her legislative attention to the west of Wells St., for example, since those living to east of Wells St. are not in the district.

The Legislature as an Institution

The Illinois Constitution outlines the duties and responsibilities of the General Assembly. Yet, like all state legislatures, it is one of the most poorly designed organizations imaginable for making the decisions necessary to fulfill these duties. Think of it. Dozens and dozens of people from every part of the state with a wide variety of personal, professional, and constituent interests meeting for several months to decide what the largest and most complex organization in the state—the state government—ought to do. The topics under consideration range from abortion to long-term health care, from pre-school education to "super-max" prisons. With an annual budget to pass the size of a Fortune 100 company and a breathtaking range of issues to consider, it is a wonder the legislature ever gets anything done.

To facilitate policy deliberation and decision-making in this unique environment, the General Assembly sets up various sub-groups in its membership—leadership and committees—to handle certain assignments. It also sets up various rules of procedure. Thus, the complexities of the legislative process largely arise in response to the legislature trying to manage its massive responsibilities as outlined by the state constitution.

The Illinois General Assembly is a **bicameral**—two-chamber—body. It consists of a Senate with 59 members and a House of Representatives with 118 members. Each senator represents a district with approximately 210,000 residents (as of the 2000 census). Because of the difference in population density in various areas of the state, some Senate districts cover vast tracks of land in several counties, while others cover only a few dozen square miles. Each Senate district is split into two House districts of approximately 105,000 residents each.

It is vital to understand that a senator or member of the House (known as a "representative") is elected by only those people living in his or her own district. To be re-elected, a member of the General Assembly must satisfy a majority of his or her constituents (or at least a majority of the constituents who vote). Thus, members from Chicago must pay attention primarily to the interests of Chicago, while members from DuPage, Sangamon, and Pope counties will have other constituents to satisfy, often with quite different interests. This arrangement sets up many clashes of interest in the legislative process, but it can also provide you with enormous insight into why members act as they do and what arguments and ideas might interest them most. The *Almanac of Illinois Politics* is an excellent source for learning some basic information on legislators and the districts they serve.

The *Almanac of Illinois Politics* is a reference book on the Illinois General Assembly that has been produced every two years since 1990 by the Institute for Public Affairs (now the Abraham Lincoln Presidential Center for Governmental Studies) at the University of Illinois at Springfield, telephone (217) 206-6502. It contains detailed information about each member of the General Assembly, including data on elections, legislative voting, and district demographics.

Legislative Sessions

The Illinois Constitution directs the General Assembly to convene on the second Wednesday of each January to consider legislation. Each General Assembly lasts for two years, beginning in the January following a general election. Under the Senate and House Rules in the first year of a General Assembly (the odd-numbered year), the legislature is intended to deal broadly with substantive, or regular policy-oriented, legislation. The second year (the even-numbered year), is reserved for the consideration of emergency or substantially important legislation. However, in practice, much regular policy is considered in the second year as well. Also, each year in the spring session the General Assembly must pass the state's annual budget—a major undertaking in itself!

The president of the Senate and the speaker of the House are responsible for developing a calendar of legislative events for each session. For example, the House calendar for April 2002 is shown on page 10. The deadlines specified in the legislative calendar are very important and bills must complete each step in the process by a certain date to remain under consideration. If a bill fails to meet a deadline, it does not proceed on the path toward passage unless given special consideration. While those deadlines impose barriers to bill passage, they also keep the process in motion and force decision-making.

The regular session is held in the spring. This is when most new legislation is proposed and when the General Assembly passes the state budget for the following fiscal year, which begins on July 1. (By contrast, the federal government's fiscal year begins October 1.) The spring session usually lasts from January until the end of May.

The fall session is referred to as the **veto session**. The veto session lasts about two weeks, with the legislature usually meeting for three days before and three days after Thanksgiving. It is held primarily for the consideration of legislation passed in the spring session but vetoed by the governor. However, legislators may still introduce and

State Legislative Districts in Illinois

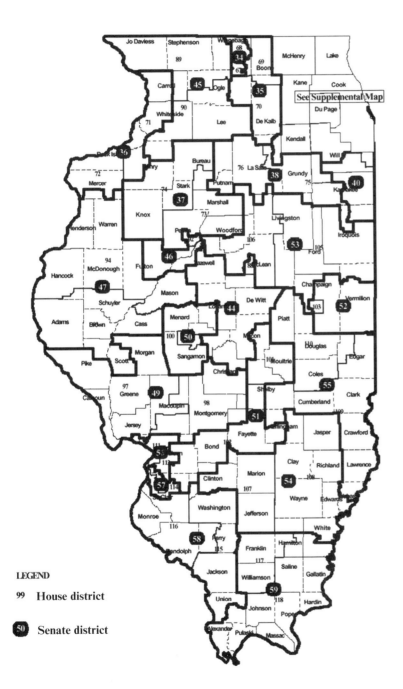

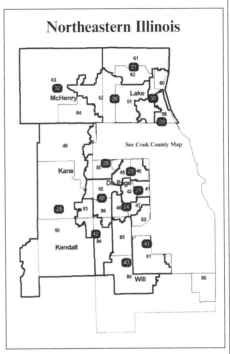

Northeastern Illinois

Cook County

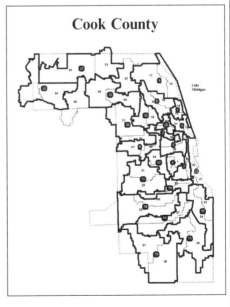

LEGEND

99 House district

50 Senate district

Every ten years, the state is divided into legislative districts of equal population, based on the decennial census. These are the districts based on the 2000 census that will be used in the 2002-2010 elections.

This is the House's legislative calendar for April 2002. The calendar indicates the days the House is in session and provides notice of two legislative deadlines.

Special session: A special session of the legislature may be called by the governor or the president of the Senate and speaker of the House jointly to deal with a very specific legislative agenda, often just a single bill or issue. A special session may be as brief as a day, but when the governor and the legislature are at odds over an issue, it may last several days or more.

First Reading: The act of the Secretary of the Senate or Clerk of the House announcing the introduction of a bill in his or her respective chamber by reading the bill's title aloud before that body. Following First Reading, the bill is sent to the Rules Committee for assignment to a standing committee for consideration.

pass new legislation during the veto session. In addition to the regular spring and veto sessions, the governor or the president of the Senate and speaker of the House jointly may call a **special session** to address a specific problem or concern.

The Path from Bill to Law

For a bill to become law, it must be considered in and passed by both legislative chambers in exactly the same form and then approved by the governor. In the diagram on page 11, the path is traced in broad outlines through the originating chamber, concurrence between the chambers, and finally to the governor's desk.

Passage in the Chambers

Bill introduction: The General Assembly can enact laws only through the passage of bills (see the Illinois Constitution, Article IV, Sec. 8(b)). When a legislator wants the

General Assembly to consider a policy idea, the idea is drafted into a bill. The **Legislative Reference Bureau** (LRB) ensures that the bill is in the proper format and reflects the current status of the law. The LRB provides the legislator sponsoring the legislation with approximately 15 (if a Senate Bill) or 12 (if a House Bill) copies of the drafted legislation. The Secretary of the Senate requires 12 copies of any bill introduced in that body, and the Clerk of the House requires nine copies of bills introduced there. The remaining copies are distributed at the sponsor's discretion.

Upon receipt from the sponsor, the Secretary or Clerk assigns the bill a number and announces it to the sponsor's chamber. This announcement is known as **First Reading**. Following ancient Anglo-American legislative tradition, the Illinois Constitution requires that all bills be read by title on three different days in

How A Bill Becomes Law in Illinois

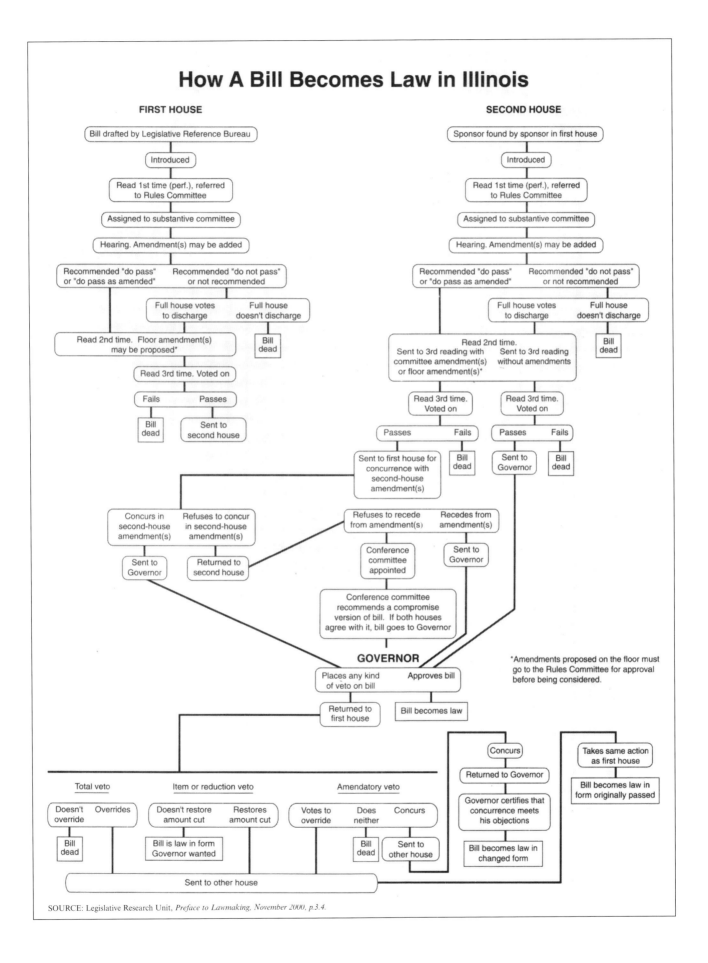

FIRST HOUSE

Bill drafted by Legislative Reference Bureau

Introduced

Read 1st time (perf.), referred to Rules Committee

Assigned to substantive committee

Hearing. Amendment(s) may be added

Recommended "do pass" or "do pass as amended" — Recommended "do not pass" or not recommended

Full house votes to discharge — Full house doesn't discharge

Read 2nd time. Floor amendment(s) may be proposed* — Bill dead

Read 3rd time. Voted on

Fails — Passes

Bill dead — Sent to second house

Concurs in second-house amendment(s) — Refuses to concur in second-house amendment(s)

Sent to Governor — Returned to second house

SECOND HOUSE

Sponsor found by sponsor in first house

Introduced

Read 1st time (perf.), referred to Rules Committee

Assigned to substantive committee

Hearing. Amendment(s) may be added

Recommended "do pass" or "do pass as amended" — Recommended "do not pass" or not recommended

Full house votes to discharge — Full house doesn't discharge

Read 2nd time. Sent to 3rd reading with committee amendment(s) or floor amendment(s)* — Sent to 3rd reading without amendments — Bill dead

Read 3rd time. Voted on — Read 3rd time. Voted on

Passes — Fails — Passes — Fails

Sent to first house for concurrence with second-house amendment(s) — Bill dead — Sent to Governor — Bill dead

Refuses to recede from amendment(s) — Recedes from amendment(s)

Conference committee appointed — Sent to Governor

Conference committee recommends a compromise version of bill. If both houses agree with it, bill goes to Governor

GOVERNOR

Places any kind of veto on bill — Approves bill

Returned to first house — Bill becomes law

*Amendments proposed on the floor must go to the Rules Committee for approval before being considered.

Total veto — Item or reduction veto — Amendatory veto

Doesn't override — Overrides | Doesn't restore amount cut — Restores amount cut | Votes to override — Does neither — Concurs

Bill dead | Bill is law in form Governor wanted | Bill dead — Sent to other house

Concurs

Returned to Governor

Governor certifies that concurrence meets his objections

Bill becomes law in changed form

Takes same action as first house

Bill becomes law in form originally passed

Sent to other house

SOURCE: Legislative Research Unit, *Preface to Lawmaking, November 2000, p.3.4.*

each chamber prior to passage. Each reading marks a key stage in the movement of a bill along the path from introduction to passage. First Reading merely conforms to the constitutional requirement of reading the title of the bill aloud in the respective chamber, serving as the official start of the legislative process.

Committee assignment: After First Reading, the bill is sent to the **Rules Committee**. The Rules Committee is responsible for assigning the bill to an appropriate standing committee for consideration. In odd-numbered years, most bills are assigned to committee. The House requires that all bills be assigned within three legislative days. The Senate has no such requirement, and either majority leadership opposition or apathy can lead to some bills languishing in the Rules Committee without ever receiving an opportunity for a public hearing.

Committee assignment is important because the members of one committee might be more favorably inclined toward a bill than those of another committee. This is because legislators are attracted to serve on different committees that best serve their constituents or interests. For example, a bill banning a pesticide would likely get very different treatment from the House Committee on Agriculture (which likely attracts legislators from farming districts) than it would from the House Committee on Environment and Energy (which may attract legislators interested in protecting the environment). For further explanation of how and why a lobbyist can

work to influence committee assignments, see Chapter 4.

An important variation in the committee assignment process is that in even-numbered years, any non-appropriations bill must be declared by the Rules Committee to be an "emergency" or "of substantial importance to the conduct of state business" to be considered by the chamber. Without this designation, the bill cannot be assigned to a committee and never receives consideration.

Committee action: Once a bill is assigned to a committee, the committee's staff members analyze and study it's content. Each **caucus**—the party organization in each chamber—has at least one staff person per committee to serve its members. These staff issue reports, called "bill analyses," to their party's committee members. These analyses briefly state what the bill would do if enacted into law, who supports it, who opposes it, and other relevant information. For further explanation, see "Working with Legislative Staff" in Chapter 5.

By order of the chairperson, the bill is **posted** for a committee hearing. Posting is the official public notice that at a specific date, time, and place, the committee will consider the bill. By rule, these notices must be posted six days in advance of the hearing. Hearing postings can be found on the Senate and House bulletin boards, located outside each chamber, the chamber's daily calendar, and the General Assembly Web site. Committee chairpersons are also required to notify all sponsors of bills appearing before the committee of the day, hour, and location of the hearing. Committee

The **Legislative Reference Bureau (LRB)** is a non-partisan support agency of the Illinois General Assembly carrying out a variety of legal and technical functions. The primary task of the LRB is to draft and prepare legislation for lawmakers and provide them with legal advice. The LRB is staffed predominantly by attorneys and paralegal professionals.

Contact Information:
Legislative Reference Bureau
112 Statehouse
Springfield, IL 62706
Telephone: (217) 782-6625

hearings are generally held in the Statehouse or the Stratton Building, which is located directly west of the Statehouse. However, hearings may be held elsewhere in the state under special circumstances or when the General Assembly is not in session. The James R. Thompson Center in Chicago's Loop often hosts such hearings and other official state meetings.

At a committee hearing, testimony may be taken from those wishing to speak on the bill. Typically, those testifying include the bill's sponsor, lobbyists both in favor and against, and officials of state administrative agencies that might be affected. Sometimes interested citizens will testify, but a lobbyist usually arranges these appearances since most citizens have neither the time nor the inclination to monitor these proceedings. See the section in Chapter 3, "Lobbying through Committee Testimony," for more details on this process.

After considering public testimony (although not necessarily the same day), the committee typically votes on the bill, recommending by a majority vote either that:

- The bill be passed by the chamber in its current form;
- The bill be passed with specific amendments approved by the committee;
- The bill be sent to a subcommittee or an interim study committee for further discussion; or
- The bill not be passed or considered further.

If no committee action is taken, the measure may be re-referred to the Rules Committee or reported without recommendation to the chamber. In either case, the bill is considered dead except under extraordinary circumstances.

Bill amendments on the floor: When a bill is reported from the committee to the full chamber, the Secretary or Clerk announces it formally. This is known as the **Second Reading**. Other than during the committee process, Second Reading is the only time that a bill can be amended in its progress through the originating chamber. After all offered amendments (if any) have

Statehouse: Common name for the Illinois State Capitol Building.

Second Reading: The act of the Secretary of the Senate or Clerk of the House announcing that a bill has been reported back to the chamber after consideration by the standing committee. While the bill is on the order of Second Reading, proposed amendments are in order, along with debate and voting on these amendments.

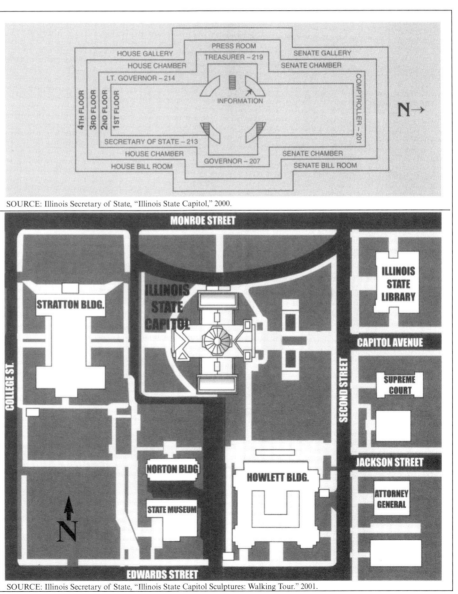

SOURCE: Illinois Secretary of State, "Illinois State Capitol," 2000.

SOURCE: Illinois Secretary of State, "Illinois State Capitol Sculptures: Walking Tour." 2001.

A diagram of the State Capitol and map of the surrounding area.

Third Reading: The stage of the legislative process in which the full chamber debates and votes on the final language of the bill. Bills cannot be amended on Third Reading.

Super-majority: A number of votes in excess of a majority sometimes required for bill passage and other legislative acts, such as overriding a gubernatorial veto.

Consent Calendar: A listing of non-controversial bills and resolutions. No debate is in order for any item on the consent calendar.

Enrolling and Engrossing: The administrative unit in each chamber responsible for incorporating any amendments into a bill after it passes the chamber of origin and before it is sent to the second chamber, and after it passes both chambers but before it is sent to the governor

This Notice of Hearing provided advance notice of the bills under consideration by the House Judiciary II- Criminal Law committee on February 18, 2001 at 10:00am in Hearing Room D-1 in the Stratton Building.

been considered and voted on by the full chamber, the bill automatically advances to **Third Reading**.

Bill passage in the originating chamber: Third Reading is the decision-making stage, when the full chamber debates and votes on the bill. The bill may not be amended on Third Reading, but the chamber may vote to return it to Second Reading for the purpose of amendment. The final roll call vote on the bill is done electronically and displayed at the front of the chamber. Bill passage requires the affirmative vote of a constitutional majority of the elected members— 30 in the Senate and 60 in the House—except for

some special circumstances when a **super-majority** is required.

Bills deemed by the legislative leadership to be non-controversial are sometimes accorded special treatment by being placed on a **Consent Calendar**. All bills on a Consent Calendar may, by unanimous agreement in the chamber, be passed on a single roll call vote, although the record will report individual roll calls. Consent Calendars increase the efficiency of the process by eliminating the need for legislators to vote on each of these non-controversial bills.

After a bill passes in the originating chamber, it goes to **Enrolling and Engrossing**, where administrative staff

The Stratton Building is located directly west of the Statehouse and houses many state legislative offices and hearing rooms.

prepare it for introduction in the other chamber. The original bill and any changes made to it in the form of amendments are combined into a single document representing the bill as it passed that chamber. This **engrossed bill** is then reported to the other chamber for consideration. Upon receipt, the bill is placed on the order of First Reading until a sponsor is identified. After a sponsor is identified, the bill is read into the record (First Reading) and automatically reported to the Rules Committee for assignment. It is vitally important for the success of the bill that a member of this second chamber be prepared to sponsor it as soon as it arrives. If such a sponsor can be found, the bill repeats the process of committee hearing and Second and Third Readings in the new chamber. Without a sponsor, the bill remains on the order of First Reading.

Concurrence by Originating Chamber and Conference Committees

Bills in identical form must pass both chambers to be sent to the governor. Therefore, if a bill is amended in the second chamber (as is often the case), it must be sent back to the originating chamber for **concurrence** on the changes. If the originating chamber votes not to **concur** with the amendments, the second chamber may vote to **recede** from its amendments.

If the second chamber refuses to recede from its amendments, leadership from each chamber may appoint a **conference committee** to negotiate a version agreeable to both chambers. If no conference committee is appointed, the bill dies. Each conference committee is comprised of five

Engrossed bill: A bill that has passed its chamber of origin and into which all of the passed amendments have been incorporated for introduction in the second chamber.

Concurrence: Agreement by one chamber of the General Assembly to an amendment added by the other chamber. Concurrence may also refer to the adoption of a joint resolution originating in the other chamber.

Concur: To agree to an amendment made by the other chamber.

Recede: To undo action previously taken, such as when a chamber agrees to retract an amendment.

Conference committee: Ten legislators, five from the Senate and five from the House, who attempt to resolve differences between versions of a specific bill or joint resolution passed by their respective bodies. The conference committee reports recommendations back to both chambers for further action.

Conference committee report: The final version of a bill negotiated by a conference committee for consideration by each chamber.

Enrollment: The processing of a bill (or joint resolution) that incorporates all amendments, if any, when a bill passes both chambers of the General Assembly. The enrolled bill is the document that is signed by both presiding officers and sent to the governor.

Appropriations bill: A bill that authorizes a named governmental entity to spend a certain amount of money from a specific source (such as the General Revenue Fund) for a specific purpose.

legislators from each chamber, with three members appointed by the majority party and two members appointed by the minority party of each chamber. Generally, the bill's sponsors are appointed to serve on the committee. If an agreement is reached by a majority of the conference committee members, a **conference committee report** is drafted and circulated by staff. The conference committee report must be signed by at least six members of the conference committee before it can be filed in each chamber. In most cases, conference committee reports must be approved by a majority of the members in each chamber. (In some cases, bills may require a super-majority. For instance, bond bills require a three-fifths super-majority rather than a simple majority for passage.) Once the conference committee report passes each chamber, it is sent to the governor for consideration. If a conference committee report fails to obtain a constitutional majority in either chamber, the process may be repeated once with each chamber appointing members to the new conference committee. Membership of the second conference committee may or may not be the same as the first conference committee.

Unlike a conference committee report, a bill that passes both chambers in the same form returns to the originating chamber for **enrollment**. All of the various amendments are incorporated into a single document that is then signed by the presiding officer of each chamber. Following the passage of a bill by both the Senate and House, the chamber of origination has up to 30 days to transmit the enrolled bill formally to the governor for action.

Conference committees sometimes change bills dramatically, even adding language never before seen in either version of the bill. Therefore, legislators may sometimes vote differently on the Third Reading of a bill than they do on a conference committee report on the same bill. In trying to understand how a legislator voted on a particular issue, you must consider the exact language of each version of the bill.

The Governor's Desk

Under the Illinois Constitution, the governor has five alternatives when considering a bill that has been passed by the General Assembly. He or she may:

- Sign the bill into law;
- Take no action, and after 60 days the bill becomes law without the governor's signature;
- Amendatorily veto the bill, suggesting specific changes in it to the General Assembly;
- Execute a line item veto or reduction veto on appropriations bills; or
- Veto the entire bill.

The governor signs the bill: A signed bill becomes law exactly in the form that it passed the General Assembly.

The governor takes no action, and the bill becomes law: A bill that has passed both chambers of the General Assembly in identical form must be presented to the governor within 30 days of its passage by the last chamber to do so. The governor then has 60 days to consider the bill. If the governor fails either to sign or to veto the bill by the end of these 60 days, the bill automatically becomes law. Although rare, this situation may occur, for example, if the governor disagrees with the bill but not strongly enough to reject or amend it.

The governor executes a line item or reduction veto on the bill (appropriations bills only): The governor may reduce (but not increase) any dollar figure in an **appropriations bill** or cut out an entire line item from the appropriation. These powers were given to the governor by the 1970 Illinois Constitution to encourage fiscal restraint in state government. Any portion of an appropriations bill not reduced or vetoed becomes law when signed by the governor (or within 60 days if no further action is taken by the governor). In response to such a veto, the General Assembly may do any of the following:

- Vote to restore (override) a reduced appropriations item by a constitutional majority vote of both chambers. If this happens, the bill becomes law with the original amount restored.
- Vote to replace (override) a vetoed line item by a three-fifths super-majority vote of the membership

of both chambers (36 votes in the Senate and 71 votes in the House). If this happens, the bill becomes law as the General Assembly originally passed it.

- Fail to override the reduction or line item veto, in which case the bill becomes law without the vetoed item or with the reduced appropriation.

Note that the reduction veto requires only a majority vote, not a super-majority vote, to be overridden. Still, it is a powerful gubernatorial tool for at least two reasons. First, appropriations bills are usually omnibus, and thus large and complex, and legislators may vote in favor of the entire

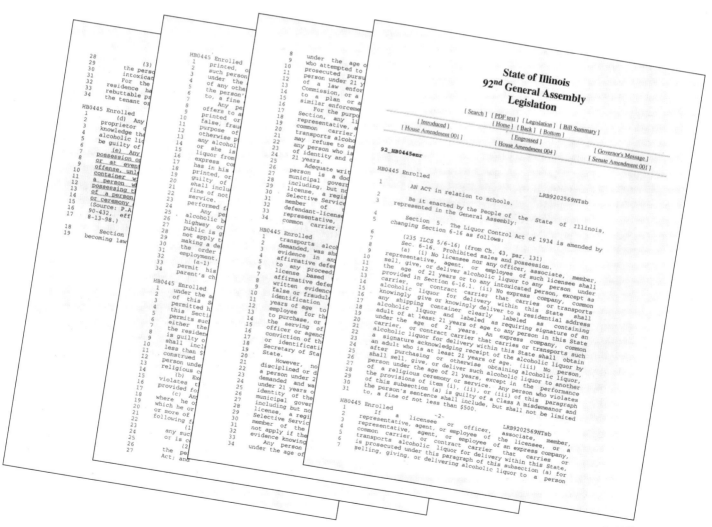

Here is the printout of the Enrolled Bill of HB0445 in the 92nd General Assembly, a bill to ban alcohol on school property. Any enrolled bill can be retrieved from the General Assembly Web site at http://www.state.il.us/statelegisl, by clicking on "Legislation- Status and Text" and then "Full Text" on the bill's summary page.

package, not necessarily approving of each individual item. So when the governor singles out one such item for reduction, it likely has less legislative support than does the full bill. Second, when the governor executes a reduction veto on an item, there is a lot of political weight and prestige behind that decision, even if informally, and media attention is often drawn to the cut. This action is often enough to reduce support for the item, at least among those whose support was initially marginal.

The governor amendatorily vetoes the bill: With an amendatory veto, the governor recommends specific changes to the bill. The governor's recommendations are contained in a **veto message** that is sent to the originating chamber. In response to an amendatory veto, the General Assembly may do any of the following:

- Override the governor's amendatory veto and reject the recommended changes with a three-fifths supermajority vote of both chambers. If this happens, the bill becomes law in the form passed by the General Assembly.

- Accept the governor's recommended changes with the appropriate number of votes, generally a simple constitutional majority of the membership of both chambers. If this happens, the bill becomes law in the form recommended by the governor.

- Fail to override the amendatory veto or to accept the recommended changes. If this happens, the bill dies.

The amendatory veto is a powerful tool for the governor because there is often a big difference between getting the additional votes required to override the veto

The governor signing a bill into law. Sometimes the governor will turn a bill signing into a public event for press coverage.

and just getting the majority needed to pass the bill with the governor's changes. Partisan competition has been so close in the state legislature in modern Illinois history that rarely has one party had a three-fifths super-majority in either chamber. Thus, even a party that controls both chambers must usually compromise with the minority party to override a veto successfully. Less obvious, but no less important, this close balance of power often gives less formal legislative coalitions, such as the Black Caucus or the Conference of Women Legislators, influence in an override fight. So the governor's amendatory veto (or even the threat of it) will often affect the politics, as well as the content, of a bill.

The governor vetoes the entire bill: By this action, the governor rejects the entire bill and returns it to the General

Four types of gubernatorial vetoes:

Total veto: The governor rejects the entire bill. A three-fifths super-majority vote of each chamber is needed to override.

Amendatory veto: The governor vetos the bill with specific suggestions for changes. A three-fifths super-majority vote of each chamber is needed to override, but only a majority vote in each chamber is needed to accept the suggestions the governor makes.

Line item veto: The governor vetoes only specific line items from an appropriations bill, allowing the rest of the bill to become law. A three-fifths super-majority vote of each chamber is needed to restore the line items.

Reduction veto: The governor reduces a specific line item in an appropriations bill by a specific amount, allowing the rest of the bill to become law. A majority vote of each chamber is needed to restore the line item to its original amount.

HB 445
Amendatory Veto

OFFICE OF THE GOVERNOR
207 STATE CAPITOL, SPRINGFIELD, ILLINOIS 62706

GEORGE H. RYAN
GOVERNOR

August 3, 2001

FILED
AUG 3 '01 -5 30 PM
SECRETARY OF STATE INDEX DEPT.

To the Honorable Members of the
Illinois House of Representatives
92nd General Assembly

Pursuant to the authority vested in the Governor by Article IV, Section 9(e) of the Illinois Constitution of 1970, and re-affirmed by the People of the State of Illinois by popular referendum in 1974, and conforming to the standard articulated by the Illinois Supreme Court in People ex rel. Klinger v. Howlett, 50 Ill.2d 242 (1972), Continental Illinois National Bank and Trust Co. v. Zagel, 78 Ill.2d 387 (1979), People ex rel. City of Canton v. Crouch, 79 Ill.2d 356 (1980), and County of Kane v. Carlson, 116 Ill.2d 186 (1987), that gubernatorial action be consistent with the fundamental purposes and the intent of the bill, I hereby return House Bill 445, entitled "AN ACT in relation to schools," with my specific recommendations for change.

House Bill 445 makes it a petty offense for any person to have alcoholic liquor in his or her possession on public school district property on school days or at events when children are present. It exempts possession of alcoholic liquor in the original container with the seal unbroken by a person who is not otherwise legally prohibited from possessing the alcoholic liquor, and possession by a person in or for the performance of a religious service or ceremony authorized by the school board.

I agree with the intent of House Bill 445. The bill applies a petty offense to possession of alcohol by any person on school property, except under limited circumstances. The current Liquor Control Act applies a Class A misdemeanor to possession of alcohol by a person under 21. The current law's additional element of being under 21 years of age may be enough to avoid the petty offense becoming the sole penalty for possession of alcohol on school property; however, to avoid any court from so interpreting these two laws I am suggesting a change. Also, the provision covering possession of alcohol at an event where children are present was intended to cover only events on school property and I suggest language to make that clear.

HB 445
Page 2

For these reasons, I return House Bill 445 with the following recommendations for change:

On page 6, line 6, by replacing "Any" with "Except as otherwise provided in this Act, any"; and

On page 6, line 8, by inserting "on public school district property" between "events" and "when".

With these specific recommendations for change, House Bill 445 will have my approval. I respectfully request your concurrence.

Sincerely,

George H Ryan

GEORGE H. RYAN
Governor

The governor sent this veto message to the House to amendatorily veto HB0445.

Re-enrollment: The final processing of a bill when the governor has reduction, line item, or amendatorily vetoed the bill and the General Assembly accepts or fails to restore the governor's proposed changes. Re-enrollment incorporates these changes. The re-enrolled bill is presented to the governor for certification.

Assembly with a veto message outlining the objections. In response, the General Assembly may do either of the following:

- Override the governor's veto by a three-fifths super-majority vote of the members of both chambers. If this happens, the bill becomes law in the form originally sent to the governor by the General Assembly.
- Fail to override the veto by getting less than a three-fifths vote in either chamber. In this case, the bill dies.

Bills that are changed during the veto process (through amendatory, line item, or reduction vetoes) require **re-enrollment** before being sent to the governor for certification. These changes are incorporated into the bill and both presiding officers sign it

before sending it back to the governor.

When a bill is signed into law by the governor, or otherwise meets the constitutional requirements for becoming law, the secretary of state assigns it a Public Act number, which becomes its shorthand title. For example, once passed, House Bill 445 of the 92nd General Assembly became Public Act 92-0507. This numbering denotes that this was the 507th bill passed by the 92nd General Assembly to become law.

Effective Date of New Laws

A bill that passes both chambers of the General Assembly before June 1 becomes effective on January 1 of the following year, unless a different effective date is specified in the body of the bill. A bill

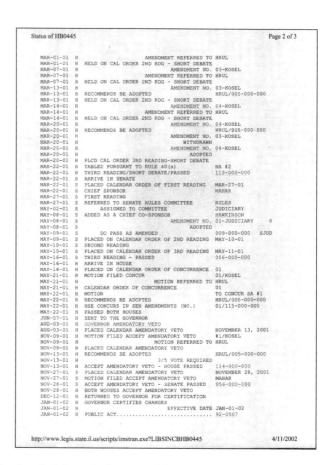

The Bill Status of HB0445 documents the legislative history of a bill to ban alcohol on school property. The Bill Status for any bill can be retrieved from the General Assembly Web site at http://www.state.il.us/statellegisl, by clicking on "Legislation- Status and Text." Test yourself by making sense of what happened to this bill at each stage of its journey through the legislature.

passed by both chambers after May 31 does not become effective until June 1 of the following year, unless an earlier effective date is specified in the bill and approved by a three-fifths super-majority of each chamber.

Constitutional Amendments

Illinois has had four constitutions since it became a state in 1818. The current Illinois Constitution was adopted in convention on September 3, 1970, ratified by a vote of the people on December 15, 1970, and became effective on July 31, 1971. The Illinois Constitution, like all constitutions, is a document that defines the fundamental structure and purpose of government. Constitutions delineate the process of governmental decision-making rather than give precise direction to specific government agencies on individual policy issues. Constitutional provisions usually have much broader impacts on the state and its citizens than do statutes. Because of this broad importance, governments generally set up especially stringent provisions for changing their constitutions. The process of amending the Illinois Constitution is no exception.

There are three ways to amend the Illinois Constitution. The most commonly used method begins in the legislature, where a resolution to submit a proposed amendment to the voters must pass with a three-fifths super-majority of the elected members in each chamber. Just as with a bill, the resolution must be read in each chamber on three different days, and it may be amended prior to Third Reading. Once passed by both chambers in identical form, the proposal is placed on the next statewide general election ballot that occurs at least six months after its legislative passage. An amendment becomes effective if approved by either a three-fifths super-

majority of those voting on the question or by a majority of those voting in the election. Thus, the governor has no official role in this constitutional amendment process, unlike the normal legislative process. In a sense, the citizens act in the governor's place, either approving or rejecting the legislature's proposal. No more than three articles of the constitution may be submitted by the General Assembly to the voters for amendment at one time.

The second way the constitution can be amended is that changes to the legislative article of the constitution may be initiated by popular petition, bypassing the legislature altogether. For example, in 1980, the voters approved the "Cutback Amendment," which reduced the size of the House by one-third and eliminated multi-member districts for that body.

The final method of constitutional amendment also bypasses the legislature, instead using a **constitutional convention** to consider and affect constitutional changes. The current Illinois Constitution requires that every 20 years the question of whether to call such a convention automatically appears on the ballot in a general election. Voters have not approved a constitutional convention since this provision was first included in the 1970 Illinois Constitution.

Ratification of an amendment to the United States Constitution requires an affirmative vote of a three-fifths super-majority in each chamber of the General Assembly (see the Illinois Constitution Article XIV, Sec. 4). ❏

Constitutional convention: A convention called to evaluate and potentially amend or rewrite the state constitution. Delegates are elected on a proportional basis from all areas of the state. The last constitutional convention was held in 1969-70 and produced the current Constitution of the State of Illinois. Other constitutional conventions were held in Illinois in 1818, 1848, 1862, and 1920.

Chapter **3**
Lobbying Essentials

In this quotation, Alan Rosenthal sums up two very important points about lobbying. First, the U.S. Constitution gives us the right to lobby public officials. You need not be embarrassed or shy when lobbying. While you should treat policy-makers with respect — which includes not wasting their time — you shouldn't feel that your lobbying activities are an unnecessary burden for them. Listening to you and your group is a big part of their job. Second, lobbying is mainly about communicating information to policy-makers. It is about educating legislators and other government officials about your group's interests and the substance and politics of the policy concerns they are charged with solving. Most policy-makers, especially legislators, are not experts on every policy concern that comes before them. They need and want the information you and your group have to offer. Your job as a lobbyist is to provide the substantive information and political context that policy-makers need to make sound decisions and to provide this information in a clear and timely fashion. In this chapter, we outline some of the basic strategies you can use to get your message across.

Monitoring Legislation

Often, groups find it is more important to prevent the passage of bills that hurt their cause than it is to introduce legislation designed to help them. To avoid being blindsided by someone else's "good idea," groups must monitor the policy-making process continually, in both the legislative and the administrative processes. Detailed steps for monitoring changes in the administrative policies of state agencies can be found in Chapter 6, Administrative Rulemaking—Lobbying State Agencies. Don't overlook the importance of this rule-making process. Agencies often have a significant impact on public policy through this process.

The first step in monitoring the General Assembly is to follow the **daily calendar** in each chamber when it is in session. If you can't be in the Statehouse every day of the session, the daily calendar for each chamber is now available online at the General Assembly Web site. Another useful source of information for bill monitoring is the *Legislative Synopsis & Digest*, which is produced weekly by the Legislative Reference Bureau. In monitoring the legislative process, pay special attention to the committees that usually handle the bills your group cares about and those bills sponsored by members who are particularly

interested in your issues (whether they are for or against your positions).

The General Assembly Web site provides an especially useful tool for monitoring legislation. On its homepage (http://www.legis.state.il.us) under "Legislation and Laws," click on "Legislation-Status and Text." This brings you to a page where you can begin searching current legislation by sponsor, bill number,

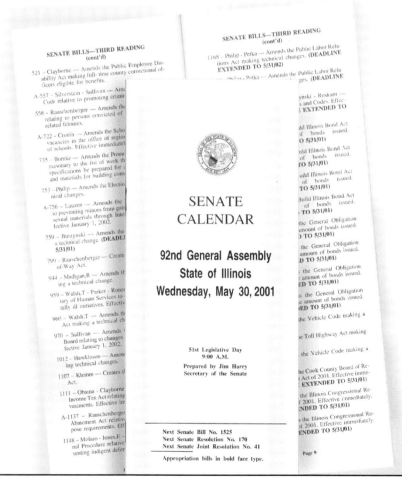

The Senate and House Calendars are produced each session day by the Secretary of the Senate and the Clerk of the House, respectively. These daily calendars track bills, and give hearing times and other information, generally outlining the events in the chambers that day. They are available free of charge at the Statehouse information desk and other places in the Statehouse.

legal citation, or topic, or simply browse bills by bill number. If you have an interest in a certain policy area or a specific section of the Illinois Compiled Statutes, you should search by the related citation regularly to see if any relevant legislation has been introduced and its status. From this Web site, you can also search legislation from past General Assemblies.

Another important tool for monitoring legislation is the **Legislative Information System (LIS)**. The LIS is a non-partisan support agency of the Illinois General Assembly responsible for providing computer services and technical assistance to its members, committees, commissions, and agencies. While the LRB is the source of information available on the General Assembly Web site, the LIS is responsible for maintaining this electronic resource. As a part of its services, the LIS has recently added customized legislative monitoring.

> " *Monitoring, broadly defined as keeping track of what policy-makers and other groups are doing, is unquestionably the most prevalent form of group political activity.* "
>
> —Nownes and Freeman (1998, 87)

This customized service lets you create files for the bills and subjects you are monitoring, allowing you to check the status of all related bills by subject at a single glance. Refer to Chapter 9 for other bill-tracking services available commercially.

These resources are invaluable for monitoring the process of legislation. Has a particular bill been assigned to a committee? What amendments were made in committee and on the floor? Has it passed Second Reading in the originating chamber? Who voted for and against it on Third Reading? This is all information you will need to update daily during session.

Know Your Legislators

An effective lobbyist knows as much as possible about the policy-makers he or she intends to lobby. This is especially important when lobbying legislators, as they are a

The **Legislative Information System** (LIS) is a non-partisan support agency of the Illinois General Assembly responsible for providing computer services and technical assistance to its members, committees, commissions, and agencies. The LIS offers a customized legislative monitoring service that allows you to create files for the bills and subjects you are monitoring, allowing you to check the of all related bills by subject at a single glance. Originally designed for use by legislators and their staff, this service is now available to the public free of charge on the General Assembly Web site.

A state senator meets with constituents in a senior center.

large and diverse group. Fortunately, it is easy to learn the pertinent facts about these very public figures. Legislators generally develop very consistent legislative records that reflect the interests of their constituents.

For biographical facts on each legislator, see the *Illinois Blue Book* or the *Handbook of Illinois Government*, both published by the Illinois Secretary of State and distributed free of charge. For more detailed information on legislative activities and district characteristics, see the *Almanac of Illinois Politics*, produced by the Institute for Legislative Studies at the University of Illinois at Springfield. Much information can also be obtained electronically at the General Assembly Web site. In addition to this Web site, each chamber and political party has its own Web site. You can also learn a great deal by reading past issues of a legislator's personal newsletter to constituents or the newspapers in his or her legislative district.

Resources for information on members of the Illinois General Assembly

Publications

The secretary of state publishes the *Illinois Blue Book* and the *Handbook of Illinois Government*. The *Illinois Blue Book* is published in even-numbered years and the *Handbook of Illinois Government* in odd-numbered years. Both are available at no cost by contacting the Secretary of State's Communications Department at (217) 782-5763.

The *Almanac of Illinois Politics* is published by the Abraham Lincoln Presidential Center for Governmental Studies at the University of Illinois at Springfield. Published in even-numbered years, copies can be purchased from the Center Publications, University of Illinois at Springfield, One University Plaza, MS HRB 10, Springfield, IL 62703-5047; Telephone: (217) 206-6502.

Web sites

Illinois General Assembly: http://www.legis.state.il.us
Senate Democrats: http://www.senatedem.state.il.us
Senate Republicans: http://www.senategop.state.il.us
House Democrats: http://www.housedem.state.il.us
House Republicans: http://housegop.state.il.us

See Chapter 9, "A Lobbyist's Guide to Information Resources," for more information.

Lobbying by Letter

One way to communicate your group's views to a legislator is by letter. This approach is easy and cheap, and it doesn't require a trip to Springfield. However, it is also the easiest approach for a legislator to ignore. A state legislator may receive dozens of letters each week. The trick is to get your letter noticed and taken seriously. Here are some recommendations for writing effective letters to legislators:

- **Timing is important**. If your letter arrives too early, it will be forgotten. If it arrives too late, there is nothing the legislator can do to help you. If the legislator is a member of the committee where your bill is under consideration, write to him or her the week before the committee holds its hearing. If the legislator is not a member of the committee handling the bill, write just before the bill is due to come to the floor for Second and Third Reading. Don't write to the members of the House while the bill is still being considered in the Senate, and vice versa. The bill may change significantly by the time it arrives from the other chamber.

- **Keep your letter short and to the point**. Except in unusual circumstances, the letter should be no more than *one page long*. Legislators are busy and don't have time to sift through a long document looking for its message. By condensing your letter to one page, you are forced to focus on the essential points of your message, and you increase the chances that it will be read.

- **Proofread carefully.** Avoid spelling and grammar mistakes, and make sure the letter appears neat and professional (word processing makes this easy these days). Don't let simple mistakes undermine your credibility.

- **Write the letter on your organization's letterhead if you are writing as a group representative**. This gives you official standing and reduces the chances of you being written off as a crank. Don't send a post card.
- **Address letters to legislators and the governor properly** (see below).
- **If you are the legislator's constituent, begin your letter by saying so**. If you supported or voted for the legislator, say that, too. These things are important to legislators and may cause them to pay closer attention to your letter. If you are not a constituent or have not voted for him or her, say nothing on these subjects.

- **Don't begin on the pompous and demanding note of "As a citizen and a taxpayer..."** The legislator assumes that you are an Illinoisan and knows that we all pay taxes.
- **Make your position clear and say exactly what you would like the legislator to do.** You get no extra points for being cute or cryptic. You greatly enhance the chances of a legislator doing what you ask if your request is clear and to the point.
- **Tell the legislator which groups and people you are working with on the issue**. But don't even imply the support of any group or person without their permission. The legislator will feel misled, and your credibility will be damaged.

An example of a letter sent to a state senator by a group lobbying for a bill. Note that it is respectful, short, clear about what it asks the senator to do, and concise in its explanation of why they want him to do it.

Address letters to legislators and the governor properly:

The Honorable Jane/John Doe
State Senator/State Representative/Governor of Illinois
Statehouse
Springfield, Illinois 62706

Dear Senator Doe/Representative Doe/Governor Doe:

March 7, 2000

The Honorable Dan Cronin
Illinois State Senate
127 Statehouse
Springfield, IL 62706

Dear Senator Cronin,

The members of the Illinois Statewide School Management Alliance respectfully ask that you support House Bill 3435, sponsored by Representative Moffitt and Senator Sieben.

The bill allows a school board to amend a certificate of tax levy when a change in the assessed valuation resulting from the Department of Revenue's application of the multiplier causes the school district's tax extensions to be less than the maximum permissive tax rate allowed by law or the maximum tax rate allowed by voter approved referendum. The amendment adopted in the House requires the district to hold a Truth in Taxation hearing prior to adoption and submission of the amended levy. The amendment adopted in the Senate makes the amended levy also limited by the Property Tax Extension Limitation Law.

As described in the January 21 edition of the Illinois State Board of Education State Superintendent's Bulletin, to reach the guaranteed per pupil amount ($4425 for FY01) school districts are responsible for a portion of the figure locally, based upon their equalized assessed valuation. If the multiplier is applied to the rate and the school district does not have access to the full amount it could result in receipt of less than the guaranteed amount.

We appreciate your careful consideration of this measure and look forward to your affirmative action.

Sincerely,

Wayne Sampson, Executive Director
IL Association of School Boards

Dr. Walt Warfield, Executive Director
IL Association of School Administrators

David Turner, Executive Director
IL Principals' Association

Dr. Ronald Everett, Executive Director
IL Association of School Business Officials

Illinois Association of
School Administrators
2020 Timberbrook Drive
Springfield, Illinois 62702
217/787-9306

Illinois Association of
School Business Officials
Northern Illinois University
1A-103
DeKalb, Illinois 60115
815/753-9368

Illinois Association of
School Boards
430 East Vine Street
Springfield, Illinois 62703
217/528-9688
630/629-3776

Illinois Principals
Association
1610 South 6th Street
Springfield, Illinois 62703
217/525-1383

- **Refer to a specific bill by name and number, and not just to a general issue, whenever possible.**
- **Write about only one bill or issue in each letter.**
- **Make the letter entirely your own**. Express your thoughts and conclusions in your own words. Don't use stereotyped phrases and sentences from form letters. They will be recognized as "pressure mail" and will not carry the impact of a personalized letter. Advise members of your group who are writing to legislators to write personalized letters, as well.
- **Your own and your group members' personal experiences are the best supporting evidence**. Tell your legislator how the bill would affect you, your family, your business, and your community.
- **Never threaten**. Don't say, "My members will never vote for you again if you don't …." In most cases, your members won't follow through on that threat, and legislators know it. While a few groups (e.g., the National Rifle Association and Planned Parenthood) have led arguably successful single-issue campaigns for and against legislators, this is very rare. These statements not only antagonize legislators, they also reduce your credibility because they reveal your naiveté.
- **Ask the legislator to state his or her position in a reply to you**. This encourages the legislator to make a commitment (although it doesn't guarantee one) and allows you to begin counting your support and opposition. Be sure to give your full name and address so the legislator can respond.
- **Write to thank the legislator.** Send a thank you note if he or she votes "correctly" on the bill, or provides other assistance, such as speaking in support of your position, introducing a bill, and so forth. Also, be appreciative of other past positive votes or actions. Legislators receive lots of mail from unhappy constituents. A friendly letter of support may be remembered favorably the next time you write.
- **Write the governor promptly after the bill has passed both chambers if you want to influence his or her decision on whether to sign it into law.**

Lobbyists and group members talk with legislators and among themselves around the "rail" outside the House chamber during a legislative session.

Remember, the General Assembly has 30 days following the final passage of a bill to send it to the governor, and then the governor has 60 days to act on it. This provides a clear time frame for your efforts at this stage of the process. The same principles for writing a good letter to a legislator apply to writing to the governor.

- **Don't send a copy of a letter addressed to one legislator to other legislators.**

Write to each legislator individually. You can write to any member of the General Assembly, but your letter will mean more to your own senator and representative. After all, they are the only ones you can vote for, and votes matter to legislators. The corollary to this is that as a group's lobbyist, you should encourage group members from as many different legislative districts as possible to write letters to their own senators and representatives. If there is a legislator you particularly need to influence, you should find someone (or more than one) in your group from the legislator's district to write a letter. Better yet, find a group member who 1) has voted for the legislator, 2) has actively supported the legislator in an election, and/or 3) works with, lives near, goes to church with, or belongs to the same club as the legislator. You get the idea. The closer the connection a letter writer has to a legislator, the more likely the legislator will read, remember, and act on it.

Some interest groups use mass mailings from group members in their lobbying efforts, but these are not nearly as effective as personalized letters from constituents. Mass mailings may be a rough gauge of citizen interest in a bill and give a group's position, but they provide no more policy information than a lobbyist can provide in a single well-written letter. Plus, legislators often see mass mailings as an annoyance, or simply as an unsophisticated attempt to apply group "muscle." Think about how you feel about anonymous and unsolicited junk mail.

Lobbying by Personal Visit

The most effective lobbying technique probably is the oldest one—lobbying legislators face-to-face. As politicians, legislators are generally very comfortable with oral communication, and they often enjoy and respond to this sort of interaction far better than they do to reports and letters. Personal discussions let them put a face to a name, assess your commitment to an issue, pepper you with questions about your group and the issue, and make a quick assessment of your character. Legislators tend to be "people people," and lobbying by personal visit takes advantage of this characteristic.

Most legislators hold regular office hours between legislative sessions at their district offices. The best opportunity for quality time with a legislator, particularly with your own legislator, is in the district office. Out of session and in their districts, legislators are often more comfortable, have more time to discuss issues, and are less overwhelmed by lobbyists and colleagues asking for help and support.

Legislators also have offices in Springfield, but because of their legislative responsibilities, they are often only intermittently available during the legislative session. Nevertheless, if a legislator gets the message that a constituent is in the Statehouse, he or she will usually come off the chamber floor, leave a committee hearing, or find some other way to meet with the constituent. The fact that a constituent has taken the time to travel to Springfield and seek out the legislator provides evidence of the level of concern. No legislator wants to be known back home for having snubbed a constituent in Springfield. And remember, you and each of your group's members are constituents of one senator and one representative. Take advantage of this fact.

Here are some suggestions for maximizing the impact of your personal lobbying visit:

- **If at all possible, make an appointment.** Don't just drop by the office unannounced. This will save you a long wait in the hall and give the legislator time to prepare. More importantly, it is just common courtesy. When making an appointment, let the secretary or legislative aide know your concern and how much time to allow for the meeting. Remember to keep it as brief as possible—10 to 20 minutes, maximum. It is also important that you don't use more time than has been allotted. Abusing a busy legislator's hospitality is not a good way to win favor. If you can't get an appointment, be prepared to talk with a legislator on the fly. Offer to accompany the legislator to his or her next destination and talk en route.

A citizen-lobbyist making his point to a state senator in the statehouse rotunda.

- **It is usually best to visit the legislator with a small group.** Three people are optimum. With more than three people, a legislator may feel threatened, and your message can get muddled. One-on-one visits with legislators may be unsatisfactory because legislators may try to out-talk you, or you may reach an impasse too quickly. In a group, you can convey the impression that you are representatives of many others, if this is indeed true. If each of you represents a different organization, your potential voting power will maximize your lobbying impact.

- **When meeting with a legislator in a small group, it is especially important that there is still one clear message.** Have at least one pre-meeting strategy session with your partners to get your stories straight. Let one person in the group be the primary speaker and contact person with the legislator.

- **If you are a constituent, introduce yourself as such to the legislator.** If you voted for him or her, say so. If you have any family, social, business, or political ties to the legislator, don't hesitate to mention them. This information will help the legislator remember who you are and better understand your perspective. However, don't assume that any connection of this sort obliges the legislator to respond in your favor.

- **Let the legislator know immediately whom you represent.** If you are working with other individuals or groups on the issue, say so. But again, don't claim an association or alliance with any group or person without their permission, even if you believe that they are sympathetic with your position.

- **Be clear about your position and what you would like the legislator to do**. Identify the bill by name and number whenever possible.
- **Give the legislator a *one-page* written statement, or Fact Sheet, of your position on what the bill does and why he or she should support your position**. While legislators tend to respond best to oral communications, they also need a written reference to a conversation. Furthermore, writing the Fact Sheet will force you to distill your arguments to their essence and make your presentation clear and efficient.
- **Be firm in expressing your position.** Don't try to force a legislator into changing positions or making a commitment if he or she clearly does not want to do so.
- **Always be calm and courteous when dealing with legislators, and never resort to harsh or personal remarks**. If you lose your temper or prevent a legislator from speaking, he or she will likely think of you as a fanatic and ignore your views.
- **To call a legislator off the chamber floor, go to the main entrance of the chamber or the appropriate side door (given the legislator's party affiliation) on the third floor of the Statehouse and give a note to the doorkeeper that explains briefly who you are and what bill you wish to discuss.** Business cards are very good for delivering such messages, but any slip of paper will do in a pinch.

For example, you might write: "Rep. Green - May I please speak with you concerning HB 563? – Maria Ortiz, Board of Education Member, School District 200." The doorkeeper will deliver your note, and the legislator usually will come out to meet with you in a few minutes.

- **To call a legislator out of a committee hearing (in emergencies only), ask one of the committee pages or the committee clerk in the hearing room to deliver your note or business card.** Wait to see the legislator's response and direction for meeting outside the hearing room.

Fact Sheet: A very brief summary (one page, usually) of your group's position on a specific bill, arguments to support this position, request for specific action on the bill (e.g., vote yes or no), your contact information, and other relevant information. Fact sheets are used in lobbying to inform and remind legislators briefly of your position and to provide arguments for your allies in legislative discussions and debate.

VOTE NO ON SB 1075

The members of the Illinois Statewide School Management Alliance urge you to VOTE NO ON SB 1075.

SB 1075 would provide an income tax credit to taxpayers for reimbursement of school tuition, book fees, and lab fees paid to any public *or non-public* elementary or secondary school. The credit would be equal to 25% of those educational expenses over $250, not to exceed $500 as a total credit for any one household.

- The actual cost of this tax credit is unknown, but it is estimated to be between $65-$150 million per year. As the legislation is drafted, it is an open-ended entitlement program without a clear funding source identified to pay for it. It is possible that home-schoolers would qualify for the tax credit, driving the cost of the program even higher.

- There is a significant concern on how to administer or enforce such a program. There is nothing in the bill that calls for verification of the cost of an individual's private school tuition or fees.

- SB 1075 would send State dollars to pay for tuition at private schools - schools that have no State accountability standards.

WE URGE YOU TO OPPOSE SB 1075

Illinois Association of
School Administrators
2020 Timberbrook Drive
Springfield, Illinois 62702
217/787-9306

Illinois Association of
School Business Officials
Northern Illinois University
IA-103
DeKalb, Illinois 60115
815/753-9368

Illinois Association of
School Boards
430 East Vine Street
Springfield, Illinois 62703
217/526-9688
630/629-3776

Illinois Principals
Association
1610 South 6th Street
Springfield, Illinois 62703
217/525-1383

Fact sheet.

Lobbying by Telephone

Telephone calls have some of the advantages and disadvantages of both letters and personal visits. Like letters, they are reasonably cheap, but they can be ignored (even if you manage to get through to a legislator directly). Like personal visits, they have more intimacy than a letter and allow for interaction, but oral arguments can be forgotten during a busy legislative session. In practice, you will use all three approaches in your lobbying efforts, with the mix depending on your resources, timing, with whom you wish to communicate, and other factors.

When the legislature is not in session, the best place to make telephone contact with a legislator is in the district office. Most legislators have offices in their home districts that can provide services and information for constituents. But if the legislature is in session and action on a bill is imminent, call a legislator at the Springfield office. In either case, be prepared to speak directly with the legislator, but don't be surprised if you are unable to reach him or her immediately or are asked to leave a message. Legislators are often out of their Springfield offices during session and may keep only certain hours in their district offices. During session they will be on the floor, in committee hearings, or at other meetings around the Statehouse. When not in session, they are out working with constituents or pursuing other aspects of their careers. Leave a detailed message with the secretary or aide stating who you are, what you want, and your telephone number. Even if you are not able to speak with the legislator directly, your message will be relayed and add to the overall impact of your lobbying effort. Most legislators will get back to you within a couple of days, especially if you are a constituent and make this point clear in your message.

You should lobby by telephone as you lobby by mail or in person—identify yourself, be clear and specific in your concerns and requests, be brief, and be polite. Here are some tips for making telephone calls to state legislators:

- **Identify yourself by name and the organization you represent (if any).** If you are from the legislator's district, give your address and hometown.
- **Identify the bill you are interested in by name and number.**
- **Briefly state what your position is and how you would like the legislator to vote or what else you would like the legislator to do.**
- **Ask for the legislator's view on the bill or issue.** Politely, try to get a commitment on how he or she will vote.
- **Show appreciation for past service or votes.** Be positive.
- **If the legislator asks for further information, supply it as quickly as possible after the telephone call.** In fact, you should drop everything to respond to the legislator's request, in full. The legislative process moves extremely fast during session. A request for information is a wonderful opportunity to

educate and persuade a legislator. You must not miss this "teachable moment." Plus, a quick and accurate response to a legislator's request shows respect and competence, enhancing your credibility.

- **Don't be abusive or threaten a legislator.**
- **Legislators can telephone you from the chamber floor during a legislative session.** If you would like to discuss a bill more fully with a legislator than you can in a brief message when the legislator is on the floor, have the secretary or aide pass along your name and telephone number and ask that your call be returned as soon as possible.

A variety of sources, both printed and electronic, provide legislator contact information, including the *Illinois Blue Book, Handbook of Illinois Government, Almanac of Illinois Politics*, and the General Assembly Web site. Other resources include: The *Roster of State Government Officials*, the *Directory of Illinois State Officials*, *Just Numbers*, and the *Handbook of the Illinois Legislature* (see Chapter 9 for additional information on these resources). Finally, during regular business hours, you can call the State of Illinois switchboard at (217) 782-2000 and ask the operator to connect you with the legislator's office.

Lobbying by E-mail

Increasingly, legislators have sites on the World Wide Web and e-mail accounts. More importantly, many legislators are actually using these resources more frequently to contact and interact with constituents, each other, and interest group representatives. While contacting legislators by e-mail may be fast and easy, it may not be the most effective means of communicating your position. While most legislators have e-mail addresses, their usage varies. To date, the traditional methods of letters, telephone calls, and personal visits are typically far more effective ways to lobby a legislator. This is especially true if you are contacting a legislator for the first time and do not know his or her style and comfort level with electronic communications.

E-mail is more ephemeral and informal than the traditional methods, and it is generally viewed as less appropriate for lobbying. However, once you establish a relationship with a legislator, e-mail may be a fast and powerful way to communicate brief ideas, strategies, and requests for help in ongoing lobbying efforts. If you do use e-mail, be sure to check with the legislator's office ahead of time to learn the communication preferences and confirm the e-mail address. There are some legislators who prefer communication by e-mail, but most do not. Still others do not have an e-mail address and have no intention of getting one.

Lobbying through Committee Testimony

After First Reading, a bill introduced in either chamber of the General Assembly is usually referred to the Rules Committee for assignment to a standing committee of that chamber. In committee, a select group of legislators hears public testimony on the bill from anyone wishing to speak. The committee then considers whether to amend the bill and what action to recommend to the full chamber. When a bill that affects you or your group is heard in committee, your interests must be represented in the form of committee testimony. See the sections on "Committee Action" in Chapter 2 for more details on the process and "Committee Strategy" in Chapter 5 to get more ideas on successful strategies. In this section, we lay out the basics of lobbying by committee testimony.

The first and most important point to remember about testifying at a committee hearing is that you need to be present at the right time and place. In most cases, you can check the current status of a bill on the General Assembly Web site to learn when and where the bill is "posted," that is, when and where it is scheduled to be heard. Notice of the bills posted in each committee is also available in the chambers' daily calendars. However, just because a bill is scheduled to be heard doesn't mean that it will be heard. Committee rules and deadlines can be suspended or changed unexpectedly. Contact the sponsor of the bill or the clerk of the committee (in the Senate, this is usually the secretary of the committee chairperson) to find out if the bill will be called for a hearing as scheduled and if testimony will be taken. Even with this precaution, you will sometimes spend long hours waiting in a hearing room for your bill to be called. But it is far better to wait a while than to cut your schedule too fine and miss your opportunity to present your case publicly to the committee.

Between the posting and the hearing, you should speak directly with the bill's sponsor about your intentions for the hearing. Perhaps surprisingly, this is especially critical for legislation to which your group is opposed. No legislator is happy about being blindsided in a committee hearing by previously unknown opposition to a bill. Remember, there are few, if any, legislators that you can afford to anger unnecessarily.

Preparation

While testifying is important and the most visible part of lobbying a committee, a great deal of work must go on long before the hearing for your testimony to be successful (see "Committee Strategy" in Chapter 5). Testifying at a committee hearing is like a play—if you don't have a good script and rehearse it well, it will be a disaster. But more important than just practicing the exact words you will say, you must know your main arguments and background information thoroughly, and you must present yourself and your "testimony team" (anyone whose testimony you coordinate, such as experts or group members) in a professional and credible manner. An average citizen's testimony can be just as effective as a professional lobbyist's—sometimes more so. But the citizen must be just as well-prepared as the lobbyist and abide by the same rules of conduct. You must organize and prepare all the members of your team thoroughly in advance.

A witness testifies before a legislative committee. Note the visual aids the witness is using to help make her case.

The most important part of preparing your testimony is defining your **lobbying message**. After brainstorming with your team or group all the possible reasons for a legislator to support your position, identify a *single sentence with no comma* that sums up your arguments. For example, "HB 2365 will improve health care for the rural poor in Illinois." Or, "SB 583 will cause some small businesses to close." Use this lobbying message as the theme for organizing the rest of your testimony. A clear focus is essential for presenting your message effectively. Develop testimony that provides factual evidence and support for this main theme.

In deciding what supporting evidence to provide for your lobbying message, determine what you can tell legislators that they don't know already. Legislators will usually know the statewide implications of a proposed law. They often get this information from state agency officials called to testify on how the bill would affect their department. But local officials, your group members, and other citizens are usually in the best position to explain how the bill will affect a specific area, community, or other segment of the state. These people have a different perspective from state agency officials and other special interest lobbyists. Lawmakers are usually eager to hear solid evidence of what a bill will really do for, or to, the people affected by it. This is where you should focus your testimony—on your unique perspective on the issue, providing stories of the specific impact on your group members. Legislators will get statewide statistics and generalities from others. It can be particularly effective to demonstrate the impact of the bill on people or businesses from the districts of committee members.

The sum of the arguments and evidence presented by everyone on your team (which, of course, may be just you) needs to support the basic lobbying message that you identified before you started. Your testimony should begin and end with this theme, and everything in between should demonstrate why that contention is true.

Attend a legislative committee hearing at the Statehouse before you present your testimony. If possible, attend a few hearings and at least one of the specific committee before which you intend to testify. This will give you a feel for how hearings are conducted, the pace of the process, the behavior of those involved, what to wear to testify, how legislators react to different witnesses, and so forth. The more familiar you are with the process, the less nervous you will be when you testify.

Even if you are sure that your battle is lost before the hearing, testify anyway and do a thorough and professional job. Your testimony may gain respect for your group and educate committee members in ways that may not be apparent immediately. Furthermore, your testimony becomes a part of the legislative record of the bill. It demonstrates that support or opposition exists. Policy-making is an ongoing process. Those who lose today may win tomorrow. Always do your best at every step of the process, regardless of the current outcome. You never know how that diligence will pay off down the road.

Written Testimony

You don't have to submit written comments with your oral testimony, but it is a good idea to do so. Some committee members may not be able to attend the hearing and, most importantly, providing a written document gives some permanency to your testimony, allowing legislators to remember and refer to what you said.

Lobbying message: The main theme of your committee testimony, supported with arguments and evidence. The lobbying message should be simple and direct, and it usually begins: "This bill will…"

ILLINOIS STATE SENATE • RECORD OF COMMITTEE WITNESS

LEGISLATIVE
MEASURE NUMBER

COMMITTEE_____ DATE_____

OTHER *(Subject matter)*_____

I. IDENTIFICATION

Name_____ Senate Dist. No._____

Address_____ City_____ State_____ Zip_____

Title_____ Firm or Business_____

Business Address_____ City_____ State_____ Zip_____

Phone_____

II. POSITION — PROPONENT

III. TESTIMONY *(Check appropriate box/boxes)*

☐ Oral ☐ Written Statement Filed ☐ Record of Appearance Only   *Signature* _____

If you wish to testify at a committee hearing, get a Record of Committee Witness forms from the committee clerk, complete it, and return it to the clerk before the hearing begins. For Senate hearings, make sure to fill out the proper slip—OPPONENT or PROPONENT—for your position on the bill.

- Prepare a short *one-page* statement of your position, similar to a Fact Sheet, but tailored to your committee testimony.
- Attach any supporting documents, such as statistical data, media accounts, case histories, or published reports, as appendices to the one-page summary. But don't go overboard. The more material you provide, the less likely it is that anyone will read it.
- Bring enough copies of your written material for each member of the committee and its staff (anticipate at least three staff people: the committee clerk and two staff analysts—Democrat and Republican). Before the hearing begins, give your written materials to the committee clerk, who is usually sitting with the committee chairperson. Also, bring copies for any members of the media who may be in the audience.

Oral Testimony

Oral testimony is the essence of a committee hearing. It is an opportunity to make your case in a public forum to those legislators most interested in the issue— the chamber's standing committee on that policy area. Be sure to practice your presentation several times in front of colleagues, group members, friends, your family, or whoever will listen. Have these people pepper you with all the questions that they can think of in response to your testimony.

- Always be certain of the bill number and subject matter. The subject of a bill may have been changed by amendment. Monitor the bill closely before the hearing to be current on any changes.
- Arrive at the committee hearing room at least 15 minutes before the posted hearing time. Get a **Record of Committee Witness form (called a "witness slip")** from the committee clerk, fill it out, and return it to the clerk before the hearing begins. This form is simple to fill out and asks only for obvious information. At this time, give the clerk any written material you would like handed out to the committee members and their staff.
- If you have submitted a witness slip, the committee chairperson should give you a reasonable opportunity to be heard. If you are overlooked, respectfully ask to speak. But be prepared to waive your oral testimony

RECORD OF COMMITTEE WITNESS

ILLINOIS HOUSE OF REPRESENTATIVES

BILL OR RESOLUTION NUMBER

COMMITTEE _____ DATE _____

OTHER *(Subject matter)* _____

I. IDENTIFICATION

Name _____

Address _____ City _____ State _____ Zip_____

Title_____ Firm/Business or Agency_____

II. REPRESENTATION *(This section to filled if the witness is appearing on behalf of any group, organization or other entity.)*

Persons, groups, firms represented in this appearance_____

_____

III. POSITION *(Check appropriate box)*

Original Bill   ❏Proponent   ❏Opponent   ❏No Position on Merits

Amendment (s) # _____ Proponent _____ Opponent _____

IV. TESTIMONY *(Check appropriate box)*

❏Oral   ❏Written Statement Filed   ❏Record of Appearance Only

Signature_____

A "witness slip" for a House committee.

if other people have already said the same things you wished to say. There is no need to annoy legislators with redundant testimony. But even if you do waive your opportunity to speak, distribute your written testimony to the committee members through the clerk.

- Dress comfortably, but conservatively. Unfortunately, your appearance may be as important to some legislators as what you say and how you say it.

- Begin your testimony by identifying yourself and giving a very brief description of whom you represent, what your organization does, and the number of members it has.

- Next, give a clear and concise statement of your position: "We are opposed to House Bill _____ and urge you to vote against it."

- After stating your position, explain your reasons. Give the political, fiscal, moral, and/or social reasons why this bill is either good or bad for the state,

depending on your position.

- Don't read prepared testimony. Provide copies of your written testimony to the committee but summarize and paraphrase that written testimony orally. This is where practicing your testimony really pays off.

- Keep your testimony brief and to the point, ideally *less than five minutes*. If you take too long, legislators start thinking about when you will be finished rather than about the content of your testimony. Supplement this brief testimony with written materials and personal lobbying of committee members, as appropriate. Five minutes isn't much time, but if you have a clear lobbying message and supporting arguments, it is enough. Practicing your testimony thoroughly is vital to keeping within this time frame.

- Be sincere, open, and honest. Most important, be yourself. Don't posture, become emotional, or engage in melodramatics.

- Keep eye contact with, and address your comments to, the committee members at all times.
- Know who are committee members and who are staff.
- Don't be surprised if some committee members talk on the telephone, consult with staff, walk away, or otherwise don't seem to pay attention to your testimony. A lot goes on during some committee meetings. Don't be flustered by all the activity. Staff and some committee members will be listening.
- If appropriate and not gimmicky, be novel in your approach. Use posters or other visual aids; conduct a brief demonstration of an activity. Legislators hear a lot of testimony and may be more likely to notice and remember something unique. But be sure to practice the use of any props or activities thoroughly in advance. You don't want legislators to remember you only because you dropped your visuals or your equipment fell apart in a comical way.

- Don't hand out written testimony while making an oral presentation. This will divert the attention of the committee from your presentation.
- Keep your language simple and non-technical. Many people at a committee hearing (including many legislators) don't understand "legalese" and the jargon of your profession or issue. On the other hand, don't talk down to the committee. Rather, speak to them as you would speak to any intelligent person who is not an expert in your field.
- Don't try to be more of an expert than you are. Don't make arguments you are not prepared to defend or prove. If expertise is needed beyond what you can provide, bring in an expert to testify as well.
- If possible, praise the general intent of the bill, whether or not you are opposed to the specific details. Otherwise, you may appear to be criticizing the motives of the sponsor and the bill's supporters. It is less confrontational to criticize the specific methods of achieving the general intent.
- Anticipate opposition arguments by challenging your opponent's statistics, assumptions, and arguments. If possible, offer concrete examples, actual case histories, or supporting data.
- Ask questions that the proposed legislation leaves unanswered.
- Mention others who support your position—but only with their prior consent.

Group members meet with a state representative to present their position on pending legislation.

- Close by thanking the committee and offering to answer their questions.
- Finally, remember that if you haven't done the preparatory legwork before the committee hearing, even the finest oral testimony is unlikely to change anyone's mind (see "Committee Strategy" in Chapter 5).

Answering Questions

As you finish your testimony, invite and be prepared for questions from committee members. This is an excellent opportunity to provide legislators with exactly the information that they need to know to make a decision on the bill. Don't feel threatened or put upon by these questions. Rather, consider this to be an excellent lobbying opportunity. In fact, it is a very good sign when a committee member asks you a question. It indicates that he or she has been listening and cares about what you have to say.

> If you don't know the name of a legislator, simply address him or her as "Senator" or "Representative." At committee hearings, this works well since you know which chamber is holding the hearing and only legislators on the committee are allowed to ask questions of witnesses.

- If possible, arrange ahead of time for a sympathetic committee member to ask you questions to help you make your points. In particular, ask him or her to give you the opportunity to rebut testimony given by the opposition, since you are not automatically granted this privilege. This is part of the important pre-hearing legwork that you must do to be successful.
- Answer all questions as honestly as you can. When you don't know the answer, say so. As needed, defer to other witnesses on your team who could answer the question, or offer to supply the information at a later date. If you do offer to get information for a committee member, make sure that you do so and deliver it personally (with copies sent to all committee members) that day or the next, if at all possible. Remember, the short legislative life of the bill continues while you are searching for this information.
- If you are asked if you would support the bill if it were amended in some way, do not commit yourself publicly unless you are absolutely sure of your group's position on the change. If you aren't sure, reply that you and your group would need to consider the amended proposal. This is not an evasive answer, but rather it is appropriate caution that legislators will understand.
- If you are asked an irrelevant or rhetorical question, use it as an opportunity to restate your position while politely diverting attention from the question.
- If you are asked a hostile or personal question, avoid a public confrontation. Diffuse the hostility by remaining unruffled and restating your position as calmly as possible. Blow off steam in private, not in a committee hearing. Regardless of what provocation you receive, an unseemly outburst from you will hurt your credibility and your cause.

Lobbying the Governor

Surrounding the governor are several layers of support staff whose function it is to find, analyze, and summarize information for the governor's consideration. These staff, located in the **Governor's Office of Legislative Affairs** and in the Governor's Office itself, can be thought of as lobbyists for a constituency of one—the governor. They work with the legislature,

Governor's Office of Legislative Affairs: The governor's staff who work with legislators, interest groups, the governor's political party, other lobbyists, and each other to protect and advance the interests of the governor in the legislative arena. Work through this office in lobbying the governor.

Contact them at:
Governor's Office of
Legislative Affairs
207 Statehouse
Springfield, IL 62706-1150

Telephone:
(217) 782-6871

interest groups, the governor's political party, other lobbyists, and each other to protect and advance the interests of their boss, while at the same time exerting as much personal influence on events as possible.

Communicate with these gubernatorial gatekeepers at each stage of the legislative process, especially if your goal is to pass a piece of legislation. After all, your hard work in the legislative process will be wasted if the governor doesn't sign the bill. You will usually work with a single staffperson whose job it is to cover your policy area (like health care or corrections). You can identify the appropriate staff member by calling the governor's office.

If your bill will be complex or controversial, you should contact the appropriate gubernatorial staffperson prior to drafting it. Bringing the governor's office in on the ground floor may give them a sense of personal investment in its eventual passage, as well as giving you early tips on potential gubernatorial objections that you may be able to work around in drafting the bill and throughout the legislative process.

If you can get the governor on record as supporting the bill early, this staffperson may help generate legislative support for the bill as it makes its way through the process, especially from legislators from the governor's political party. Maintaining contact with this staffperson throughout the legislative process is vital even if the governor doesn't go on the record as supporting your bill. This continuing contact may make the staffperson feel somewhat obligated to lobby the governor for you if he or she has been telling you all along that the bill is "okay." In addition, the staffperson may tip you off about what might be needed either to convince the governor to sign the bill or to get it passed over a gubernatorial veto. The governor's office can often be a very important source of political information— use it if you can.

The governor's office on the third floor of the Statehouse.

When a bill passes the General Assembly, a member of the governor's staff prepares an analysis to help the governor in his or her decision to sign or veto it. The analysis will address such questions as:

- Whom does this legislation affect, and how?
- What is its legislative history?
- What are the political implications of its enactment or veto?
- What are the fiscal implications of the bill? Who pays for it and from what source?
- Does the bill contain mandates to local units of government?
- Does it impose a tax?
- What are the positions of the relevant state agencies?
- What are the positions of relevant private interest groups?
- What implications does the bill have for any publicly expressed position of the governor?

If you have kept the governor's staff informed of your position throughout the legislative process, the chances are very good that at least the spirit of your concerns will be mentioned in his or her analysis to the governor. Regardless of the extent of your staff contact before bill passage, you must still present your case to the staffperson before he or she writes the analysis. At the very least, you should supply the staffperson with a Fact Sheet tailored to the governor's office. That Fact Sheet should describe what the bill does, who supports it, why you support it, and why the governor ought to sign it into law. This should be done in addition to the letters you send to the governor and any personal lobbying you are able to do with the governor's staff.

These same suggestions apply when trying to convince the governor to veto a bill. Many a bill has died at the end of the governor's pen as the result of effective lobbying. However, it is far easier to kill a bill quietly in the legislative process than through a very public gubernatorial veto. By the time a bill has reached the governor, it has gained the support of a majority of both chambers of the General Assembly, so your battle is much tougher. ❏

The Ten Commandments of Lobbying

1. Never lie or mislead a legislator about the facts of an issue, its relative importance, the opposition's position or strength, or any other matter.
2. Look for friends in unusual places. In politics, a friend is someone who works with you on a particular issue, whether Democrat or Republican, liberal or conservative. A friend on one issue may oppose you on every other issue.
3. Never cut off anybody from permanent contact. Don't let a legislator (or another lobbyist) consider you a bitter enemy just because you disagree. Today's opponent may be tomorrow's ally.
4. Don't grab credit. What you and your group want from the process is public policy in line with your interests. Legislators and others may want the public credit. Let them have it. Nothing is impossible if it doesn't matter who gets the credit.
5. Make your word your bond. Don't make promises you aren't positive you can keep.
6. Don't lobby opponents who are publicly committed to their position. It wastes your time, and it alienates them further. It is more productive to support your allies and lobby legislators who claim to be keeping an open mind.
7. Always notice and thank everyone who has helped you. People like to be appreciated and it costs nothing to say, "Thanks!" A person who feels unappreciated will probably not help you again and may even go out of his or her way to hurt you.
8. Don't gossip. Knowing legislators' peculiarities and peccadilloes is one thing; talking about them is another. If you get the reputation of telling everything you know, you'll soon find that no one will tell you anything.
9. Do your homework. There is no excuse for not having the facts and figures to support your case when you need them. It makes you look unprofessional and reduces your credibility.
10. Be there. You can know your opponent; you can develop imaginative and reasonable compromises; you can burn the midnight oil to digest all the arguments. But you have to be in the right place at the right time to win the day.

Adapted from Illinois State Support Center, *Manual of Public Interest Lobbying in Illinois*, Springfield, IL (1984), p. 7.

Chapter **4**
Legislative Process and Rules— Working Effectively in the System

As outlined in Chapter 2, the state legislature is a complicated organization governed by complex and arcane rules of procedure. These rules are designed to allow the legislature to accomplish its very difficult mission of setting policy for the large and diverse state of Illinois. Similar to the rules in games and sports, those who know the rules well can often use them to their advantage and those who don't may lose unnecessarily. A clear understanding of the legislative process and rules will allow you to make the best case for your cause and maximize your chances of winning in the legislative arena.

It would be impossible to describe all the legislative rules in detail and explain how they might be interpreted in every circumstance. Instead, we try to highlight the most common situations when knowledge of legislative rules can make all the difference. As you gain

The Handbook is published for each new General Assembly and contains a variety of useful information, such as the legislative rules, members' telephone numbers and addresses, committee assignments, and floor seating charts.

experience around the Statehouse, you will learn more specifics and tactics. As every veteran lobbyist will tell you, there is always something new to learn. These rules are largely the same from General Assembly to General Assembly, but important details sometimes change. So you must pay close attention and keep current.

The Basics of Legislative Rules

At the beginning of each General Assembly, the president of the Senate and the speaker of the House propose rules for adoption by the members of their respective chambers. These rules spell out parliamentary procedure, timetables, voting requirements, and much more. Copies of the Senate and House Rules are posted on the General Assembly Web site and are available in print from the Senate and House Bill Rooms. Other sources of these rules include: the ***Handbook of the Illinois Legislature***, ***Senate Journal***, and ***House Journal***.

A lobbyist must have at least a working knowledge of the rules because they explain in detail the process by which a bill becomes a law. As a lobbyist, the goal

Handbook of the Illinois Legislature: Contains pertinent information about both the Senate and the House, including their respective rules. It is compiled and published by the Secretary of the Senate and the Clerk of the House. Copies are available from the Senate Journal Room (Room 407 Statehouse) and the House Bill Room (Room 402-A Statehouse).

Senate and House Journals: Produced by the Secretary of the Senate and the Clerk of the House, respectively. These journals are kept daily and document each chamber's activities. Both journals are accessible by date on the General Assembly Web site. Copies are also available from the Senate Bill Room (Room 406 Statehouse) and the House Bill Room (Room 402-A Statehouse).

2001-2002
Handbook
92nd General Assembly
ILLINOIS LEGISLATURE

*The Rules
of the Senate
and the Rules
of the House of
Representatives
are adopted and
published at the
beginning of each
General Assembly.
They are posted on the
General Assembly Web site
and available in print from the
Senate and House Bill Rooms.*

of passing a bill into law (or preventing the passage of a bill) is completely dependent on this process. Failure to meet a deadline or to draft an amendment correctly can—and often does—mean the difference between lobbying success and failure.

Legislative rules are another tool—along with your general knowledge of the legislative process, good public policy arguments, and group membership—to help win support for a bill you favor or to defeat a bill you don't favor. For example, to be given a hearing, committees are required to post notice of bills. An alert lobbyist, noticing that this requirement has not been met, can kill a bill by pointing this out to a legislator-ally. Likewise, a lobbyist whose bill is failing on a critical floor vote might ask a legislator-ally to change a vote from yes to no, which under the rules permits that legislator to make a motion later to reconsider the vote. This gives the lobbyist more time to round up the required number of votes.

Always keep in mind this caveat about legislative rules: Rules can sometimes be changed. Since legislative rules are merely conveniences agreed upon in each chamber to get the

work done, and not statutes or administrative rules, a majority in a chamber may elect at any time to waive any of its own rules temporarily. While you should never count on being able to get a chamber to ignore its own rules, you should be vigilant to avoid being blindsided by an opponent who manages to circumvent the rules.

Bill Introduction

While it takes plenty of advance preparation to make it happen, the introduction of a bill is the start of the official legislative process, as governed by the legislative rules. Here are some tips on how the rules regarding bill introduction may help or hinder your lobbying efforts:

- **Bills must be introduced in a chamber by a member of that chamber.** Therefore, you need a legislator who is willing to sponsor and introduce the bill (see the next section for more discussion of sponsors).

- **Deadlines are placed on bill introductions and other aspects of the legislative process so as to keep the process in motion**. The Senate president and the House speaker establish the deadlines for bill introduction in their respective chambers prior to or at the start of the spring legislative session. The deadline may be as early as mid-February for a regular spring session and varies for appropriations and non-appropriations bills. Know what the introduction deadline is in each chamber for each spring session, and get your bill introduced on time. Bill introduction deadlines make it vital to prepare well in advance of the session. There are also deadlines throughout spring

Senate and House Rules. One of the responsibilities of the president of the Senate and the speaker of the House is to propose rules for conducting their respective chamber's business within the framework of the Illinois Constitution. These rules are adopted by the members of each chamber. The Senate and House Rules are posted on the General Assembly Web site (http://www.legis.state.il.us/) and are available in print from the Senate Bill Room (Room 406 Statehouse) and the House Bill Room (Room 402-A Statehouse). Other sources containing the Senate and House Rules are the *Handbook of the Illinois Legislature* and the Senate and House *Journals*.

Keep a close eye on the legislative calendar and do your best to get your work done well in advance of any pertinent deadlines.

session for bills to be heard in committee, passed out of the originating chamber, considered in the second chamber, and so forth. These deadlines are laid out in the **legislative calendar**, which is prepared prior to or at the beginning of each session. Get this calendar as soon as it is published and make note of these deadlines.

- **The Illinois Constitution permits the introduction of any bill in either the Senate or the House.** It costs a legislator nothing to introduce a bill. Bills are often introduced for reasons other than their sponsors' desire that they be passed that session. For example, a legislator might introduce a bill to appease a constituent or lobbyist, but have no intention of truly pursuing its passage. From a lobbyist's point of view, introducing a bill that is certain not to be approved in that session may still be useful in developing the political and educational groundwork with legislators and the public that will help it pass in a future session. Once a bill is introduced, it becomes a concrete issue for discussion and lobbying. A lobbyist can push for a committee hearing, talk it up with group members and other interested parties, obtain media coverage, and otherwise begin to inform the public about the idea. *Rarely does a bill become law the first time it is introduced.*

- **Different bills with the same intent (and even the same language) may be introduced independently.** For strategic purposes, you may want to

> The *legislative calendar* is determined by the leadership of each chamber and provided to the membership at the beginning of each session. It outlines the various legislative activities and the specific deadlines in the process. These deadlines are different in the Senate and House. The legislative calendars are available on the General Assembly Web site and printed for distribution by the Senate and House Bill Rooms.

have legislators introduce different bills reflecting various versions of an idea. More commonly, you will find other bills have been introduced with similar language. Rather than fighting with potential allies over bill details and credit, it is usually best to work together toward the common goal. This often requires delicate diplomacy to get the various factions to unite behind one bill that incorporates the best ideas of the others, thus maximizing its chances of passage. In such an instance, remember that while lobbyists are generally concerned about the final policy outcome, legislators tend to focus on getting credit for the bill's passage.

- **Sometimes the same (or similar) piece of legislation is introduced in both chambers at the same time.** This allows advocates of the policy to work in both chambers, potentially speeding up the process and increasing the possibility of passage. However, this strategy is definitely not recommended for newcomers to the legislative process. It requires skill, diplomacy, and experience with the legislative process, its politics, and especially its personalities.

- **The lack of limits on the number of bill introductions and the presence of introduction deadlines gives rise to a device used frequently by legislative leaders and other veterans—the shell bill.** A shell bill makes an extremely minor, non-substantive change to an existing statute that the sponsor intends to amend on Second Reading or in the other chamber with a more substantive amendment. This device is used to meet the deadline for bill introduction and yet allow its supporters more time to craft its content. However, it is best not to count on using such an obscure procedure, but rather to work straightforwardly, having the full bill prepared and introduced before the introduction deadline. The importance of shell bills for most lobbyists is the potential for amendments beyond the original intent of the bill. As a result, shell bills are monitored closely for both friendly and hostile amendments.

- **The large number of bills introduced each session may sometimes cause legislative leaders to limit the number of bills each legislator can move to Third Reading**. Lobbyists need to be alert to these informal rules and consider their implications when selecting a sponsor. For example, a legislator may sponsor your bill, but may not place it high on his or her priority list.

Finding the Right Sponsor

Each bill must be introduced and moved through the legislative process by a sponsoring legislator, even though the original idea usually comes from other sources, such as lobbyists, constituents, or administrative agencies. The **chief sponsor** is responsible for all official decisions connected with the bill—when to call it for a vote in committee, which amendments to allow, and how to gain support for the measure. *As a general rule, you should clear in advance all activities in support of a bill with the chief sponsor.* Tread slowly until you get to know the legislator who is sponsoring your bill. There is no better way to alienate a sponsor than to spring a surprise about a decision or activity around the bill.

Other legislators may sign on to a bill as co-sponsors, but co-sponsors generally do not make decisions about a bill's progress. Co-sponsors are often useful to show broad support for a bill, not only by the sheer number of co-sponsors (which may number as many as the entire chamber membership), but also by their legislative identities. Their partisan ties, their association with leadership, their district locations, their politics, and their reputations in the chamber send signals to other members about the bill. For example, a bill whose co-sponsors are from both parties and cover a variety of geographic areas and ideologies is probably non-controversial and a safe yes vote for most members.

Identifying a Potential Sponsor

In searching for the right chief sponsor for your bill, look for someone who will not only introduce the bill, but someone who will also be committed to it and work hard for its passage. The right sponsor may have some of the following characteristics:

- **Your local senator and representative**. They may know you, trust you, and want to please you. This increases the chances that they will agree to sponsor the bill and work for its passage. This is especially true if your group has strong ties to the area.
- **A legislator whose district is affected positively by the bill**. Such a member will get electoral benefit from sponsorship and thus has an incentive to work hard. For example, a legislator from Chicago can tout sponsorship of a mass transit bill in an election brochure, just as a member from downstate Macoupin County can claim credit for a bill to assist farmers.

- **A legislator who has introduced such a bill previously**. Chances are that he or she has a territorial interest in the subject and wants to continue being identified with it. In fact, not approaching such a legislator first with the idea might be considered offensive.

- **A legislator who has expertise in, and is deferred to on, the subject by other members**. For example, only a few legislators are considered experts on the school aid formula, and other legislators tend to trust their leadership on the issue. These legislative experts often sit on the committees that deal with the issue, are legislative veterans, and have sponsored similar legislation previously. You can identify such issue leaders by asking legislators and your fellow lobbyists.

- **A member of the committee to which the bill will likely be assigned, preferably its chair or minority spokesperson**. Committee members respect one another's bills and routinely pass them out of committee, which is a critical step in the process.

- **Someone in the party leadership**. While party leaders are busy, the extra clout they have in the process makes the effort to get one of them on board as a sponsor for your bill worthwhile. This is especially true for a leader who has some of the other characteristics of a good sponsor.

- **Someone who has great personal appeal in the legislature**. Conversely, avoid members who are not well liked or respected by their peers. A bill, especially a minor bill, may be voted for or against by some members simply because they like or dislike the sponsor (and a bill that is minor to some members may be life or death to

you and your group!). Observation and discrete inquiries will help you classify legislators on this characteristic.

- **A legislator supported by your proponents and allies**. For example, a legislator who has received campaign contributions from the education lobby and sponsored bills on special education might agree to sponsor your bill to increase school taxes because the special education cooperatives support it.

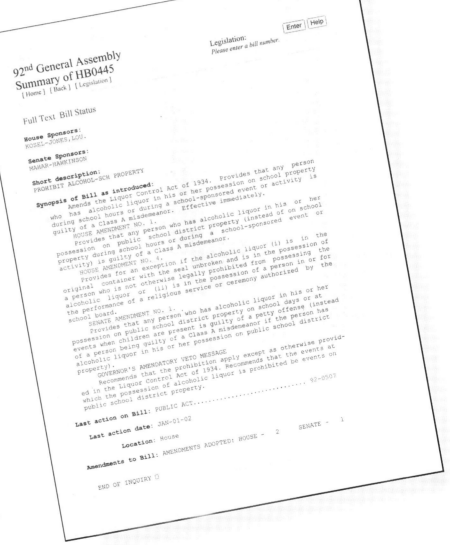

In this Bill Summary of HB0445 taken from the General Assembly Web site, note the names of the House and Senate sponsors. The chief sponsor in each chamber is identified first, followed by the chief co-sponsors. On the Web site, these sponsors' names are linked from this bill summary to a list of other bills they have sponsored.

• **A legislator supported by your opponents**. This may require more persuasion on your part than asking a natural ally to sponsor your bill, but it can pay off greatly in the long run by defusing the opposition. On the other hand, such a sponsor may not work aggressively for your cause for fear of alienating traditional supporters.

• **Someone in the governor's political party**. This will make it easier for the governor to sign your bill into law, should it get that far.

Note that the best sponsor for your bill probably incorporates many of these characteristics. In fact, it may be obvious to you after considering the membership of the chambers and the history of your issue that only one or two legislators would make the best sponsor. The more of these characteristics that describe a member, the easier it will be for you to convince him or her to sponsor the bill and work aggressively for passage, and the easier it will be to get the bill through the process.

Since a bill must pass both chambers to become law, you need to find a good sponsor in each chamber. To find the right person in the initial chamber, start doing your homework and sounding out potential sponsors in the fall before the legislature convenes in January. Begin the process of lining up a sponsor in the second chamber before your bill passes out of the first chamber. Work with the sponsor you already have to identify and secure a sponsor in the second chamber.

Securing a Sponsor

Once you have identified a legislator who will make a good sponsor for your bill, you must convince him or her to sign on. You need to make a thorough case to the potential sponsor and have all your information ready in advance. You will need to answer all of the questions he or she will have about the bill, including:

• What is the substance of the bill, and why is it needed?

• Who will be for it, and who will be against it?

• Which groups, interests, and regions are hurt and helped by it?

• What was the fate of similar bills in the past?

• What are the strengths and weaknesses of potential proponents and opponents?

• How much will the bill cost to implement, and where will this money come from?

• What are acceptable compromise positions?

• Do any other states have similar legislation?

• How will sponsoring the bill benefit the legislator? Will it specifically benefit his or her constituents? Will it generate favorable publicity?

• What can and will you and your group do to help pass the bill?

The more information you can supply the legislator, the stronger your pitch will be. Not only will the information itself help the legislator make a reasoned decision, but the fact that you are prepared and professional will lend confidence that you know what you are doing. A legislator does not want to get involved with incompetent groups that will not pull their own weight in the legislative process or, worse, that will prove to be an embarrassment through poor work or alienation of constituents and legislators.

You should provide the potential sponsor with a draft of the proposed bill, or at least an outline of what you would like the bill to contain. The Legislative

Reference Bureau (LRB) will prepare the bill for introduction, but the closer your draft is to the correct form, the greater are the chances of seeing the bill drafted the way you want it.

You may not be the best person to approach your potential sponsor initially, especially if you do not know the member personally or have some other connection. In such cases, find out as much as you can about the legislator's background (for example, from the *Illinois Blue Book* or the *Almanac of Illinois Politics*) so that you can identify an appropriate contact person. For example, an officer or important member of your group from the legislator's district might make a good contact person, or perhaps someone who is a strong supporter or long-time colleague or friend of your potential sponsor. Ideally, you will brief this contact person on your proposal and accompany him or her to make your pitch to your potential sponsor.

Working with Your Sponsor

Once you convince a legislator to introduce your bill, your work has only just begun. From the time you first approach a legislator about sponsoring your bill until the end of session, you should remain in close contact, keeping that legislator informed about your activities and where you can be reached on short notice. Your sponsor will likely have 20 to 50 other bills that he or she is sponsoring, co-sponsoring, or otherwise interested in during the session, and your bill may not have a very high priority. For your bill to have any hope of legislative success, you must do most of the behind-the-scenes work for your sponsor. You must coach your sponsor on the arguments for and against the bill, find a sponsor in the other chamber, prepare and distribute Fact

Working with the Legislative Reference Bureau

Legislative proposals, whether bills, amendments, resolutions, or conference committee reports, are usually drafted by the Legislative Reference Bureau (LRB). Senate and House staffers also draft legislation occasionally, but they generally limit themselves to amendments with minor language or technical changes. The Bureau of the Budget prepares the governor's budget proposal and may draft appropriations bills. But the LRB is where most of the bills you promote will be drafted. In working with the LRB, remember these simple suggestions:

- Be prepared. Know what you want the bill to do, what sections of the compiled statutes might be affected, and so forth. Have as many specifics as possible to expedite the process and gain the confidence of the LRB staff.
- See the *Guide to Drafting Legislative Documents* on the LRB's Web site (http://www.legis.state.il.us/commission/lrb/lrbguide.htm) for detailed information on this subject.
- Deliver the bill language to the LRB in hard copy and in electronic format, on disk or as an e-mail attachment.
- Allow plenty of time for drafting. Demanding a rush job at a busy time of the year (e.g., the beginning of session) will not endear you to the LRB nor will it likely expedite your request. Bills may be pre-filed anytime between November 30 and the opening day of the new session.
- Demanding that specific language be included in the bill will generally make the process less efficient. Allow the legal staff the leeway to do its job, translating your idea into the proper legal language.
- Along with your bill draft or memo, give the LRB a concise and precise synopsis of the bill. Draft this accurately, putting the bill in the best light. If you do a good job in drafting this synopsis, it may be used on the cover of the bill. A bill's official synopsis is extremely important, since during the hectic days late in the session, it may be all that many legislators read prior to voting on the bill.

The office of the Legislative Reference Bureau is located on the first floor of the Statehouse.

Sheets, generate media support and coverage, provide technical data for committee hearings, testify at hearings, organize coalitions, lobby other key legislators, and write speeches for yourself, your members, your sponsor, and whoever else might help your cause, among other things. Perhaps most importantly, you must serve as your sponsor's eyes and ears in identifying unexpected opportunities and problems. The more support you can provide for your bill and your sponsor, the greater are the chances of your bill passing.

Rules Committee

The Rules Committee in each chamber is a permanent committee consisting of five members. Three members are appointed by the presiding officer (the president or speaker) and two by the minority leader of each chamber. Members serve at the pleasure of their respective party leaders. The President of the Senate and the Speaker of the House along with the minority leaders are eligible for appointment to the Rules Committee. Members meet upon notice by the chairperson, usually the majority leader of the chamber. The Rules Committee is the only committee that may meet while the chamber is in session. Because of its membership composition and key role in processing legislation, the Rules Committee in each chamber is one of the important ways in which party leaders, especially majority party leaders, exert control on the legislative process.

In odd-numbered years, all bills are automatically referred to the Rules Committee after introduction for assignment to a standing or special committee. In the Senate, the Rules Committee may be selective and choose not to assign certain bills. By chamber rule, the House Rules Committee must refer all bills to a standing or special committee within three legislative days of introduction.

In even-numbered years, the Rules Committees of both chambers are more selective in the bills they refer to standing and special committees. Bills assigned to committee are limited to appropriations bills and bills deemed by the Rules Committee to be emergency measures or to be of substantial importance to the operation of government.

The Rules Committee is also responsible for referring all floor amendments, joint action motions for final action, and conference committee reports. A governor's executive reorganization orders are also automatically referred to the Rules Committee for assignment to a standing committee. Chamber rules vary on the handling of resolutions.

The Rules Committees may also re-refer a legislative measure from a committee to a Committee of the Whole or to any other committee at any time. Under certain circumstances, a legislative measure referred by the Rules Committee to a standing committee may be heard by that committee with only a one-hour advance notice. Legislative measures that fail to meet required deadlines are re-referred to the Rules Committee unless certain qualifications are met.

See the Senate and House Rules for more specific details on the Rules Committees.

If your proposal succeeds and the bill is signed into law, quietly step into the shadows and allow the sponsor the full media spotlight and credit. You and your group want the policy; let the legislator get the public credit. A legislator for whom you helped get good publicity will consider you a friend for a long time.

Finally, when the session is over and you have either won or lost, express your appreciation to the sponsor for his or her work on the bill. Gratitude freely given is appreciated; perceived ingratitude may never be forgotten or forgiven. Even if you feel that the sponsor didn't do everything possible to help you, he or she may have a different perception of the experience. You may need to call on this sponsor again in the future to re-introduce this bill or another one. State policy-making is an ongoing, never-ending process. You should always be laying the groundwork for future legislative action.

Committee Assignment

Each chamber has its own **Rules Committee**, which, among other things, assigns each bill to a single **standing committee** for consideration after First Reading. Often, the subject matter of a bill could lead to it being assigned to one of several committees. For example, a House bill about using cigarette tax revenue for anti-smoking advertisements might be assigned to the Revenue Committee (because it deals with taxation), to the Health Care Availability and Access Committee (because it deals with a health issue), or to the Children and Youth Committee (because it aims to prevent children from smoking).

Thus, the assignment process is sometimes subjective, and matters other than the subject of the bill may influence it.

If there is any uncertainty about where your bill may be assigned, the sponsor should ask members of the Rules Committee to send it to the committee most likely to act favorably on it. This can be the difference between a bill getting a fast and friendly hearing and its being ignored and forgotten. As a lobbyist, you should know the standing committees and their members, investigate the possible assignment options, and work with the bill's sponsor to have it referred to the friendliest committee.

Once assigned, a bill can be reassigned to a different committee by the chamber leadership or by a majority vote of the whole chamber. This is unusual and much more difficult than influencing the initial assignment. But if you find yourself in a hostile committee, you haven't much to lose by attempting it.

Spring sessions in even-numbered years are meant to deal mainly with the budget and emergencies, so the Rules Committee assigns to standing committees only those bills it declares to be "**emergency measures**," that is, bills necessary for the conduct of state affairs. However, like committee assignments, this is a subjective decision that can be influenced by effective lobbying.

Committee Action

Standing committees screen the large number of bills that are introduced in the legislature each year, sort out those that are meritorious and have a chance of passing into law, contribute to the legislative record of a bill with public hearings and debate, and modify bills to increase their chances of passing on Third Reading. Committee notices of a bill's hearing must be posted on the bulletin boards outside each chamber and appear in each chamber's daily calendar. Committees must post hearing notices at least six days in advance. Notices are also sent to each sponsor and co-sponsor. On the appointed day, the sponsor decides whether to call the bill for a hearing. The sponsor may determine that the timing is not right for hearing the bill and delay it until the next committee meeting.

At the bill's hearing, the sponsor makes an opening presentation in support of the bill. The sponsor may make the entire presentation or just a very brief statement and then turn the microphone over to a lobbyist or other expert for further explanation. In either case, when the committee finishes questioning the sponsor, it may allow anyone in attendance who signs a witness slip and registers an opinion the opportunity to speak (see "Lobbying through Committee Testimony" in Chapter 3). This is the time for those who oppose the bill to raise their objections. It is also common for officials of executive agencies that may be affected by the bill to address the committee. Thus, it is always advisable to discuss your bill with the relevant agency officials before the committee hearing. You may be able to resolve their concerns or at least develop effective counterarguments.

During the hearing, members of the committee may suggest specific changes to the bill. Likewise, the sponsor or other witnesses may offer amendments. The committee votes on proposed amendments as they arise. The sponsor makes any concluding remarks before the final action. A vote by the committee is then taken to make any of the following recommendations to the full chamber:
- Do pass;
- Do not pass;

Standing committee: A group of legislators from the same chamber of the General Assembly organized for the purpose of performing certain legislative functions, and to consider and decide on the disposition of legislation in a certain area of law. *Standing committees are the public forums of the legislature.*

Emergency measures: Bills necessary for the conduct of state affairs. To be assigned to a standing committee by the Rules Committee in even-numbered year regular sessions, a non-appropriations bill must be deemed by the Rules Committee to be an emergency measure.

- Do pass as amended;
- Do not pass as amended;
- Do pass (as amended) and be placed on the Consent Calendar;
- Do pass (as amended) and be placed on Short Debate Calendar (House only);
- Tabled (House only);
- Be not approved for consideration (Senate only); or
- Without recommendation.

While these are just recommendations to the full chamber, anything other than "do pass" (with or without amendment) usually means the bill will likely not pass the chamber that session. The committee may also decide to hold the bill in committee, refer it to a subcommittee, or place it on the interim study calendar. These actions postpone the bill's progress and may result in its early death, but there are options you can pursue to keep it alive (see below).

Facts and Figures

Fact Sheets

Legislators consider hundreds of bills each year. They receive an overwhelming amount of information on these bills, everything from constituent letters to newspaper articles to discussions over lunch with colleagues. An effective lobbyist gets information to legislators in a form that can be read quickly and digested easily, and with clear relevance to the actions necessary. The best way to present your case is with a well-written Fact Sheet (see "Lobbying by Personal Visit" in Chapter 3).

A Fact Sheet should be no longer than one page. It should identify the bill by number, state what action is requested, give a *brief* explanation of why it is needed, and (in even-numbered years) explain why the bill is an emergency and needs immediate legislative attention. The information must be accurate and footnoted to its original sources, as appropriate.

It is best to hand out Fact Sheets personally rather than mailing them. They make excellent summaries of your key points that you can leave with a legislator after a personal visit to reinforce your position or hand out to committee members and staff before you testify. Indeed, hand them out to anyone in a position to have a positive impact on your bill, including journalists. The more widely these summaries of your arguments are distributed, the more likely it is that they will inform the debate on the issue. Staff often adapt a well-prepared Fact Sheet for the bill analyses they write for legislators of their party prior to consideration in committee and on the floor.

Fiscal Notes

A **Fiscal Note** estimates how much a bill will cost to implement. Whenever a bill may have fiscal implications for the state,

---

If your bill fails in committee...

If your bill fails to get a favorable recommendation or is held in committee, ask your sponsor to consider these options:

- File a motion with the Secretary of the Senate or Clerk of the House to take the bill from the table and place it on the order of Second Reading. This must be done within two legislative days after the bill is reported out and requires a majority vote in the chamber.
- Re-introduce the bill under different sponsorship, if the bill introduction deadline has not passed.
- Amend the bill onto another bill.
- File a motion with the Secretary of the Senate or Clerk of the House to discharge the bill from committee. This requires a three-fifths vote of the membership in the Senate and a majority vote of the membership in the House.
- Work with the Rules Committee to get the bill re-assigned to a more favorable committee.

the sponsor may be requested by one of his or her colleagues to provide a Fiscal Note from the board, commission, department, agency, or other affected entity. Once a Fiscal Note is requested, a bill cannot be advanced from Second Reading until it is provided. Opponents may purposefully wait until you are ready to move the bill to Third Reading before requesting a Fiscal Note. Such a late request acts as a delaying tactic, preventing the bill from meeting the deadline required for passage and defeating the measure without a roll call. State agencies are allowed five days to respond to Fiscal Note requests, but they may request additional time.

It is important to pay close attention to your bill's Fiscal Note for two reasons. First, the question of cost is foremost in many legislators' minds when considering a bill. Any bill requiring funding affects the state budget and raises questions as to how the measure will be financed. All things being equal, a bill that doesn't cost the state much will pass more easily than one that costs a lot of money. So there is an incentive to keep the estimate of the fiscal impact as low as possible. The

This Fiscal Note was completed by the State Board of Education because the bill relates to the School Code. Like many Fiscal Notes, this one is vague in its cost estimate due to the uncertainty of predicting such impacts.

Legislative Notes required for some bills

- **Fiscal Note**: An estimate of the potential immediate and long-range costs for state and local government of a non-appropriations bill, requested by the bill sponsor from the state agency most directly affected.

- **Pension Impact Note:** An estimate of the impact on the public pension system of a bill that amends the Illinois Pension Code, requested by the Secretary of the Senate or Clerk of the House from the Pension Laws Commission.

- **Judicial Note:** An estimate of the need for a change in the number of judges proposed in a bill, requested by the bill sponsor from the Illinois Supreme Court.

- **State Debt Impact Note:** An estimate of the impact on state debt of any bill authorizing long-term debt or appropriating money from bond financing, requested by the chairperson of the Rules Committee in the bill's chamber of origin from the Illinois Economic and Fiscal Commission.

- **Correctional Budget and Impact Note:** An estimate of the impact on the prison population and the Department of Corrections' budget of a bill that proposes a new crime, lengthens possible imprisonment for a current crime, or requires mandatory imprisonment, requested by the bill sponsor from the Department of Corrections.

- **Home Rule Note:** An estimate of the impact of a bill that proposes to deny or limit any power or function of a home rule unit, requested by the bill sponsor from the Department of Commerce and Community Affairs.

- **Balanced Budget Note:** An estimate of the impact on the overall budget of a proposed supplemental appropriation, prepared by the sponsor usually with the help of the Bureau of the Budget.

- **Housing Affordability Impact Note:** An estimate of a bill's immediate and long-range impact on the cost of a single-family residence, requested by the bill sponsor from the Illinois Housing Development Authority.

- **State Mandate Note**: An estimate of the fiscal impact of a state mandate on local governments, school districts, or community college districts, requested by the bill sponsor from the Department of Commerce and Community Affairs (for local governments), the State Superintendent of Education (for school districts), or the Illinois Community College Board (for community college districts).

Adapted from: Legislative Research Unit, *Preface to Lawmaking*, November 2000, p.8.3-8.6.

second reason to pay close attention to the development of the Fiscal Note is that, like all forecasts, whether economic or meteorological, they are subjective and difficult to make with accuracy. To make matters worse, the state agency that calculates the Fiscal Note may oppose your bill. If so, the agency may inflate its cost estimate in an effort to prevent the bill's passage.

Consider the following hints for using Fiscal Notes effectively in lobbying:

- Have cost data available even before you ask a legislator to sponsor the bill. He or she will want to know the costs involved when you request sponsorship. Prepare a Fiscal Note yourself before the bill is introduced.

- When preparing your own Fiscal Note on the bill, refer to the appropriate House or Senate rules on Fiscal Notes and the related statute, the Fiscal Note Act (25 ILCS 50/1-9), for additional information.

- Be the first one to prepare a Fiscal Note on the bill. This places the state agency or your opponents on the defensive by forcing them to rebut your facts and figures. In the case of a new program for which data are sketchy or unavailable, your Fiscal Note may become accepted as the true estimate of cost.

- If possible and appropriate, offer to work with or consult the state agency officials preparing the Fiscal Note on the bill. They may not necessarily be opposed to the bill and may welcome your help.

- Give your Fiscal Note to the standing committee and Appropriations Committee staff. Providing staff with accurate, well-presented information helps them explain your position and your message.

- Sympathetic Appropriations Committee staff may help overcome an erroneous or inflated Fiscal Note from the opposition. You can also challenge an agency's figures through a sympathetic legislator.
- Lobbyists opposing a bill can also use a Fiscal Note, especially if they believe the cost of a program has been underestimated. Prepare a Fiscal Note as part of your opposition strategy.

While Fiscal Notes are the most recognized, there are a number of other notes that are required for particular types of bills and work in the same fashion as the Fiscal Note (see previous page). Check to see if any of these notes apply to your bill. If so, make sure that the notes are requested by the sponsor and filed in a timely fashion so that passage is not delayed.

We refer to sections of the Illinois Compiled Statutes (the state laws) as follows. A statute cited as 25 ILCS 50/1-9 is Chapter 25 of the Illinois Compiled Statutes, Act 50, Sections 1-9.

Amendments

It is rare that a bill of any importance passes through the legislative process and into law as it was originally introduced. The amendment process is an essential part of lawmaking. This is how a bill is crafted to meet the political and policy needs of the state as legislators, lobbyists, and executive agency officials consider and comment on it's provisions.

A bill can be amended as many times as needed, in committee, on the chamber floor, and even on the governor's desk. But two constitutional provisions limit the acceptability of amendments:

- Bills and amendments must be confined to one subject, and appropriations bills must be limited to the subject of appropriations. While this

The Illinois Supreme Court building is directly across Second Street from the Statehouse. In recent years, the Supreme Court has interpreted the single subject rule for legislation more strictly, going so far as to invalidate major legislation that it felt covered more than one subject.

Single subject rule: Article IV, section 8d of the Illinois Constitution states that "Bills, except bills for appropriations and for the codification, revision or rearrangement of laws, shall be confined to one subject." In other words, bills must deal with a single subject of law, with the noted exceptions. The Illinois Supreme Court is the final arbiter of whether a law is "confined to one subject."

Germane: Relevant or appropriate. An amendment must be germane to the bill that it amends. Whether an amendment is germane to a bill is the decision of the committee chair or presiding officer.

Enacting clause: The phrase in a bill that formally expresses the legislative sanction of the General Assembly. The enacting clause follows the title and is a necessary part of every bill. The phrase is, "Be it enacted by the People of the State of Illinois, represented in the General Assembly..."

single subject rule has often been ignored by past General Assemblies, recently, the Illinois Supreme Court has interpreted this provision more strictly, going so far as to invalidate major legislation because it covered more than one subject.

- To avoid having to be read on three different days in each chamber, an amendment must be **germane**, or relevant, to the original subject matter of the bill.

In practice, these constitutional mandates have been interpreted to mean that an amendment must amend the same chapter of the Illinois Compiled Statutes as the original bill.

A key to effective lobbying is using amendments freely and creatively. From the beginning of the legislative session, you need to consider how you can achieve your policy goals both by allowing your own bills to be amended and by amending the bills of others.

First, you will be faced with strategic decisions about the extent to which the bills you are advocating can be amended without sacrificing their value. In other words, how much are you, your sponsor, and your allies willing to compromise? You need to anticipate these decisions at every stage of the process. Sometimes you can use compromise to your advantage. For example, you may include preferred, but not essential, provisions in your original bill as potential bargaining chips for later legislative negotiations. You may anticipate committee members' potential objections to your bill and prepare compromise amendments in advance to meet their objections. This will give the appearance of your being both willing to compromise and professional, thus enhancing your bill's prospects. But just as important, you need to determine your

bottom line. At what point would you rather kill your own bill than see it passed in a modified form?

Sometimes you will need to compromise with a competing interest group to move your bill. Legislators do not like to pick winners and losers, and when they find themselves between rival groups, they become frustrated. Such a situation often leads to a bill's death, so it is usually incumbent on the group that wants a change to compromise more than the group that prefers the status quo. If you and your opponent can work out a compromise, legislators are often happy to go along with it.

You can also pursue your policy goals by amending bills other people have introduced. However, an unwritten rule of etiquette in the legislature is that a bill's sponsor should be consulted before proposing an amendment to the bill. Essentially, the sponsor gets the right of first refusal for offering an amendment. If the sponsor refuses to offer your amendment, you may then look for a more sympathetic legislator.

There are two basic approaches to amending other people's bills. First, if your bill is defeated at any stage of the process, consider the following options:

- Persuade the sponsor of a related bill to agree to have some or all of your bill's language tacked on as a friendly amendment.
- Identify a shell bill that has been successfully moved some distance through the process and convince the sponsor to amend it with your bill's language.
- Change a related bill in the second chamber with a minor technical amendment and plan to have the original sponsor refuse to concur, causing the creation of a conference committee. Through the conference commit-

tee, you and your legislative allies may be able to add your bill's language as an amendment to the conference committee report.

Second, you can also use the amendment process to kill, weaken, or improve a bad bill that someone else has introduced:

- Amend the bill to delete the **enacting clause**, so that even if passed, it can never be enacted.
- Amend the bill to strike sections that hurt your policy interests.
- Amend the bill to make it so bad or extreme that it won't pass.
- Amend language onto the bill so that its sponsor will kill it rather than have it approved.
- Amend the bill to delay its implementation with a distant effective date or add a sunset provision (see the next section).

Because this sort of "killer amendment" is often obscure and difficult for the public to understand, you can sometimes convince legislators to vote for them even when, for electoral reasons, they would not vote against the bill itself.

Also, remember that just as you are trying to amend other people's bills, other people will be trying to amend your bills to fulfill their policy goals. Make sure that your sponsor informs you immediately of any such attempts (remember that the sponsor has the unofficial right of first refusal). This is another important reason to keep a close and strong working relationship with your sponsor.

Effective Dates

If you oppose a bill that appears headed for passage, you might try amending it to include a postponed **effective date** or a **sunset provision**. Unless otherwise stated in legislation, bills passed before June 1

Effective date: The date on which a Public Act takes effect and is generally enforceable.

Sunset provision: The date on which a Public Act is no longer in effect and is no longer enforceable.

Senate hearing room located in Room 212 Statehouse, previously the chambers for the Illinois Supreme Court.

become law on January 1 of the following year, and bills passed after May 31 become law on June 1 of the following year. To override these defaults, bills may also specify a date on which they become effective. For example, to put off the detrimental effects of a bill, try amending it with a distant effective date, perhaps one or two years in the future. Conversely, if you can convince legislators that a program or policy is experimental with an uncertain long-term impact, you may be able to amend the bill to include a sunset provision, that is, a date after which the law will no longer be in effect. For example, the following language specifies a sunset provision: "Section 3 shall be effective through December 31, 2007." A sunset provision may also be used as a compromise to facilitate bill passage. Opponents might be willing to go along with a "pilot program" or "limited-term policy." Once a program has been implemented and had several years to prove its usefulness, it may stand a better chance of permanent legislative approval.

Floor Debate

While most bills that reach the floor ultimately pass the chamber because of the diligent work of sponsors and lobbyists, sometimes floor debate and floor votes are crucial to the passage and final form of a bill. Floor debate can be especially important when:

- The gallery is filled with constituents, interest groups, or media representatives who collectively create public pressure on legislators' votes; or
- A bad bill can be made to appear ludicrous or nonsensical by using extreme arguments in debate.

Unfortunately for you, a lobbyist loses control of a bill when it is debated on the chamber floor. To have input into floor debate and floor activity, you must organize legislators in advance who will make key arguments and generally speak in support of the bill. Try to line up legislators from different camps to demonstrate the bill's broad support. For example, a conservative suburban Republican and a moderate downstate Democrat announcing support for a bill sponsored by a liberal Chicago Democrat shows members who aren't familiar with your bill (which will be most of them) that there is no major opposition and that it is a safe "yes" vote. But you must select these legislators carefully, just as you selected your sponsor carefully. No matter how knowledgeable or supportive a member is, if he or she has a bad reputation or tends to alienate colleagues, then thank him or her for the vote, but don't ask for a speech on the floor.

An effective lobbyist ensures that legislator-allies do not enter a floor debate without sufficient relevant information not only to make the arguments in favor of the bill, but also to counter any negative arguments. Sponsors and allied speakers need to be briefed thoroughly and in a timely manner. Also, the more coordination among these members that you can achieve, in terms of who will speak when and who will make which points, the better the outcome. Keeping in close contact with the respective committee staff is also essential.

Although the role of floor debate is usually negligible in influencing legislators' votes, it is important in establishing legislative history. All action on the floor of both chambers is recorded verbatim. Amendments added on the floor are debated during Second Reading, and the debate on Third Reading is immediately before the final vote on the bill. This legislative history may become important in subsequent legal or administrative interpretation of the law and in future legislative action on the subject. Thus, you must present your case effectively and thoroughly on the floor, whether you win or lose.

Courts often look for **legislative intent** in interpreting the law. Therefore, an effective lobbyist tries to orchestrate the floor debate so that a legislative history favorable to his or her position is recorded in the **transcript**. The safest and most straightforward way to accomplish this is to write a script for two or more legislators that includes a question-and-answer dialogue clearly delineating the bill's scope and meaning. If you are planning to challenge the bill in court, careful management of floor debate may force a bill's supporters to make admissions that later can serve as the basis for the legal challenge.

If your bill fails to get the required number of "yes" votes for passage on Third Reading, its sponsor may ask that it be placed on the **Order of Postponed Consideration**. This request is granted as a matter of privilege by the chamber as a whole, but it is only available once per bill. To qualify for postponed consideration, the bill must fail with no less than two-fifths of the vote (24 in the Senate, 47 votes in the House). If you feel that the vote on your bill will be close, discuss this option with your sponsor in advance. If postponed consideration is requested, your sponsor should request a copy of the roll call (which is available only to the sponsor) immediately after the vote. Use this roll call to identify and lobby members voting "no" before the bill comes up for another Third Reading vote in that chamber.

Conference Committee

For a bill to pass from the General Assembly to the governor's desk, both chambers must approve it in identical form. If the second chamber amends the bill and the originating chamber refuses to concur with the changes, and if the second chamber refuses to recede, the bill's sponsor in the originating chamber may request the creation of a conference committee. A conference committee consists of members of both the Senate and House appointed by their respective majority and minority leaders to work out a compromise between the two versions of the bill. This compromise is then voted either up or down in both chambers, with no opportunity for further amendment.

Conference committees are generally created during the last hectic days of a legislative session, and they present an equal opportunity for victory and defeat. In theory, the committee is supposed to concern itself only with the points of disagreement between the chambers on the bill. In fact, they can completely rewrite the bill if they so desire. Bills reported by conference committees typically pass the chambers, and since their reported bills cannot be amended, you must work hard to influence the conference committee to the greatest extent possible.

If your bill requires a conference committee, work with the sponsor to influence which legislators are appointed to serve. In the end-of-session frenzy, it is often difficult to locate the time and place of conference committee meetings, so it becomes crucial to have an ally appointed to the committee who can keep you informed of its actions. Once the committee is formed, talk with each of the members about your position before their first

Legislative intent: The purpose for which a bill is introduced or passed. Legislative intent is usually more or less subjective and open to argument, and it can be important in judicial and administrative interpretation.

Transcript: A record of the actual floor debate in the Senate or the House on a legislative day, consisting of what is spoken by each legislator.

Order of Postponed Consideration: A procedure that allows a bill that has failed by no less than two-fifths vote on Third Reading to be voted on again later in the session. This procedure is available only once per bill.

meeting. Indeed, sometimes conference committees don't even meet as a group, working instead through aides, memos, and telephone calls. Thus, it is important to contact these legislators as soon as you know who they are. Just as important, identify the legislative staff working with the committee and offer them your information and assistance. Because of time constraints, staff members usually write the conference committee report, so your good relationship with them is crucial.

If the conference committee report fails to pass either chamber, the entire conference committee process may be repeated once. But often, the session ends before the process can be repeated.

Veto Overrides

Once your bill has passed both chambers in identical form, it is sent to the governor (see sections in Chapter 2, "The Governor's Desk," and Chapter 3, "Lobbying the Governor"). If the governor signs your bill, break out the champagne because your bill is law and will become operative on its effective date. However, if the governor vetoes your bill in some way, you will have to work hard to have any hope of salvaging it.

First, get a copy of the veto message from the Governor's Office of Legislative Affairs and discuss your strategy for the fall veto session with the bill's sponsor. If the governor amendatorily vetoes your bill, you might decide to ask the General Assembly simply to approve the changes the governor recommended. Such approval requires a majority vote in each chamber, but since the bill already passed both chambers, you probably will not need to do much additional lobbying. The General Assembly usually goes along with a sponsor's request to approve an amendatory veto.

However, if the governor's changes would do significant harm to your bill, or if the governor vetoed your bill outright, you need to consider with your sponsor whether you are willing to make the effort to obtain the three-fifths super-majority in each chamber required for an override. Overriding a gubernatorial veto is very difficult. Even if your bill received a large majority upon passage in the spring session, the factors influencing legislators' decision-making during the fall veto session are sometimes very different. For example, the veto session occurs after the November election in even-numbered years, but before new members have taken their seats. Thus, there may be several **lame duck** legislators voting on your bill, and even returning members worry less about re-election at this time than in the spring of an election year. The simple fact that the governor vetoed your bill raises all sorts of issues for legislators that have nothing to do with the bill itself but involve their relationships with the governor or their understanding of the governor's veto powers.

Since the governor vetoes bills in mid-summer after the spring session, and the legislature doesn't convene its veto session until late October or November, you generally have a few months to organize your veto override efforts. The first step is to examine the governor's veto message closely to understand the objections. Of course, these objections may be just public rationalizations for decisions that were made for other, perhaps political, reasons. For example, even if it is true, the governor won't write in the veto message, "I vetoed this bill as my revenge on Senator X for not voting for my road package." Instead, the message may refer to the expense of the proposed program or to how other laws are already taking care of the problem.

Regardless of whether the message contains the real reason for the veto, you can often use it as the basis for your override strategy. Rather than making the full case for your proposal to legislators yet again, focus your override arguments on the reasons the governor presented in the veto message. That is, put the veto message to work creatively. For example, if the governor says the state can't afford the $1.5 million your bill requires, and a week later the state comptroller reports the state has a $600 million surplus, you can argue the fiscal situation has changed and the state can now afford your worthy program. If the governor's veto message suggests that the problem the bill was meant to address is not really so severe, you can mount evidence to show the urgency of the problem.

Should the vote on an amendatory veto override be close, and if you want the governor's version of the bill more than you want nothing at all, discuss the following delicate approach with your sponsor. As a roll call on the override is taken, have your sponsor judge whether three-fifths of the chamber are likely to vote in your favor using the headcount you develop in advance. If not, the sponsor can make a quick substitute motion to approve the governor's changes (with only a majority vote), thus salvaging most of the bill. ❏

Legislators debate the merits of a bill on the House floor.

Chapter **5**
Lobbying Tactics and Strategies

I n this chapter, we discuss a variety of ways you can augment and enhance the basic lobbying approaches we described in Chapters 3 and 4. Not all of these lobbying tactics and strategies will be appropriate for every lobbyist on every bill in every political situation. Some of these will enhance your long-term effectiveness as a lobbyist, and some may give you short-term advantage on a specific bill. But by reviewing them all, you can assess which will be most appropriate in a given situation.

policy-making process, the best arguments and information in the world will not lead to success in the state legislature.

There are many ways to achieve access. Some lobbyists and groups gain access through campaign contributions, others through the importance of those they represent, and still others through a reputation for technical expertise. In this section, we describe a variety of ways to achieve access. The best approach for you depends on the resources you and your group bring to the process.

Access: Being able to see a person with some influence in the legislative process at the right time. Access is about having your telephone calls answered and returned and getting the appointment you need when you need it. Having access means getting a decision-maker to hear you out, regardless of the outcome.

Access—Getting Your Foot in the Legislative Door

Access is being able to talk to a person with some influence in the legislative process at the right time. Without at least some access, lobbying is impossible. A lobbyist needs access not only to legislators, but also to their staff, allied lobbyists, committee clerks, agency personnel, campaign contributors, and doorkeepers. Access is about getting your foot in the door to sell your point of view. Only after you gain access to a decision-maker can you present your best policy arguments. Without access, without the ear of those who influence the

The Personal Connection

Identifying a personal connection to a legislator or other person in the process can sometimes help develop access. This involves finding out what experiences you and that person share and using that common bond as a conversational icebreaker. Are you both from the same town or county? Did you attend the same high school or college? Do you belong to the same religious denomination? Do you belong to the same organizations, clubs, synagogue, or church? Did you serve in the same branch of the armed forces? Do you have friends or acquaintances in common? Are you fans of the same team?

Are you a former legislative staffer?

These commonalities show the legislator that you are not a stranger and that you share similar interests and experiences. It gives you something to talk about, some point of contact beyond your policy concerns. In discussing these points of personal connection, you will be seen more as a peer and not just someone who is constantly asking for something. Springfield can be a lonely place during session, especially for new legislators away from home and family. A friendly face with something in common is often very welcome.

Of course, you don't want to push this sort of connection too hard toward building a working relationship, as its basis is tenuous, at best. In some situations, raising this sort of commonality may even be resented. Tact and a good sense of the propriety of the situation are needed in using this approach to gaining access.

Serving Legislators

Just as legislators and other policy-makers may serve your group by promoting your policy interests in various ways, you and your group may be able to help legislators. For example, legislators are often asked to help solve their constituents' individual problems, even if these problems have nothing to do with the state legislature. You and your group may be able to help a legislator solve some of these problems. Let legislators know where your expertise and influence lie and offer to help as needed.

Legislators also appreciate help in reaching their constituents, especially during the campaign season. You may be able to provide a favorable venue where a legislator can speak to and interact with your group members and other voters. Opportunities that lead to favorable media coverage for a legislator are especially appreciated. A traditional way of doing this is to give a legislator an award at a group meeting or dinner. A "Legislator of the Year" or other award (memorialized in a plaque that the legislator can display on his or her office wall) shows your appreciation for past actions and cements a bond

Legislators appreciate the opportunity to speak to local groups.

between the legislator and your group for the future. Favors like this for legislators can enhance your access to them tremendously down the road.

Using Group Members to Develop Access

Legislators try very hard to keep their constituents happy, whether out of a sense of duty or just a desire to get re-elected. The fundamental power of many broad-based interest groups in the political arena is that their members are these constituents. These group members/constituents often care, or can be motivated to care, a great deal about policy-making. As potential voters, a legislator's constituents almost always have carte blanche access. Legislators know (or believe) that refusing to speak with a constituent will have broad implications beyond just that single constituent as that person will tell family, friends, and co-workers about the experience. Identify well-spoken group members who are constituents of key legislators and work with them to lobby their senators and representatives.

Elections and Their Influence on Access

You can use the importance politicians place on elections to increase your access. Two approaches are: 1) turning up the heat on political issues you care about, and 2) helping legislators secure re-election. The first approach encourages legislators to pay attention to your issue and your position, and the second approach serves to ingratiate yourself to them, enhancing access in the future.

Legislators are acutely aware that every position they take and every vote they cast may affect the number of votes they receive in the next election and even

whether they are challenged and by whom. As an election draws near, each controversial vote assumes added significance, a fact a lobbyist can use to gain access. If you can heighten the controversy surrounding an issue, legislators will feel the need to listen to all points of view on it. They may even feel pressured to support your position simply because their constituents are paying attention. Periods immediately before primary and general elections are especially sensitive.

This is a high-stakes tactic. It is best used only when you feel both that your opposition is gaining the upper hand in the process and that the general public favors your position. Usually, reducing controversy on your bill and helping slide it through quietly is the preferred approach.

Another tactic that can enhance your access is lobbying through or with important campaign contributors. People on whom a legislator depends for financial support will have easier access than you do as a lobbyist. Find out who contributes to your targeted legislators by reviewing their **campaign disclosure reports**. If you or your group has any connection to any of these contributors, you can seek their assistance in lobbying your legislators.

People Power

Constituent pressure generated by community groups and interested citizens is a legitimate and often effective lobbying tool. By banding together to demonstrate organized support for, or opposition to, a specific bill, relatively few citizens can have lobbying power disproportionate to their actual numbers. Unless a legislator

Campaign disclosure reports: Reports that candidates and their campaign committees must file periodically with the State Board of Elections showing the sources and amounts of their campaign funds. These reports are public and can be searched at the State Board of Elections Web site.

Illinois State Board of Elections Web site:
http://www.elections.state.il.us/ The Illinois State Board of Elections maintains an interactive Web site with information on elections, election law, campaigns, and campaign finance. This site is invaluable for understanding candidates' finances and their contributors.

is moved by compelling political considerations or personal ideology on a bill, sometimes just a handful of constituents can influence his or her vote and other actions in the process. By stimulating constituent pressure, you can enhance your access to legislators. If legislators think that you represent an active and interested group, whether large or small, they are more likely to talk to you than if they think your group doesn't know or care about what goes on in Springfield.

Constituent pressure is most effective early in the legislative process. It is important to lock legislators into supporting the position you are advocating before they have an opportunity to commit themselves publicly.

Constituent pressure comes in many forms, including the traditional techniques of letter writing, personal visits with legislators, telephone calls, and committee testimony, discussed in Chapter 3. Other lobbying strategies using constituent pressure include:

- Forming a special group or committee in your community to deal with the issue. This might become the basis of a permanent coalition (see below).

- Organizing a petition drive to demonstrate mass support for your position.

- Mobilizing local officials, business people, clergy, school officials, and other community leaders to speak out on the issue. Perhaps circulate a letter addressed to the legislator that these leaders can all sign.

- Organizing a mass demonstration in a visible place to attract attention to the issue. To increase the impact of such a demonstration, encourage the local media to cover the event, and time it for their convenience (e.g., if you want the event covered by the local TV station, hold it at least two or three hours before the next news broadcast).

The power of constituent pressure highlights the value of maintaining regular communication and activities with the group you represent. As the group's lobbyist, an important part of your job is to educate members about their policy interests and the legislative process. Ideally, your group members will be well versed in methods of generating pressure and ready at a moment's

Groups often give legislators awards to show appreciation for their support and to cement ties for future work together.

notice to act as you direct them. See Chapter 7, Lobbying and Grassroots Politics, for more details on this subject.

Media Campaigns

Cultivating the interest and support of the local and statewide media can help your lobbying efforts in three ways. First, if you can convince them to adopt your point of view on an issue and run stories and editorials from this angle, legislators will hear the arguments not only from you (an admittedly biased source), but also from the more objective news media. This gives you and your information credibility, and it reinforces understanding of the issue from the most favorable perspective. Second, keeping your issue in the news creates the appearance of urgency and a groundswell of public support, increasing its practical and political significance. Thus, good media coverage can lead to legislators wanting to hear what you have to say and believing you when you say it. Third, seeing sympathetic items in the media helps boost the morale of your group members and allies.

A coherent media campaign should be an integral part of your overall lobbying strategy. Start by thinking carefully about the content, location, and timing of the media coverage you would like to see on your issue, and then pursue activities that will help achieve this ideal. This may mean that you will try to minimize press coverage until the bill arrives at a certain stage in the process, or that you will only target the hometown newspapers of a few critical legislators. The key is to customize your media campaign to the needs of your issue in a particular legislative session.

When you want to influence or gain access to a legislator, focus on his or her home district media. Not only will the legislator read, see, and hear these reports personally, it will also generate interest and shape opinion about the issue among

A letter to the editor is a traditional and inexpensive way of getting your group's ideas and opinions into the public discussion.
SOURCE: *State Journal-Register.*

his or her constituents. Tactics for targeting legislators through their local media vary with the type of district. The media in Chicago, for example, have far more resources and clout than the media in Effingham, and, therefore, they are far more difficult to influence. On the other hand, Chicago is the hometown for many more legislators than is Effingham, so the extra effort it may take to have your point of view reflected in the Chicago media may be worthwhile. A representative of a rural downstate district will have many small newspapers and radio stations in his or her district, all of which need to be tapped in your media efforts.

Plan your media strategy before the legislative session begins, but allow flexibility to respond to events as they happen. In doing so, consider a variety of approaches to gaining and shaping media coverage of your issue:

- A traditional way of using the local press is through "Letters to the Editor." These can alert readers to the issue, convince readers of your position, demonstrate that there are responsible and articulate people who hold your position, and enlist others to engage in lobbying. Helping a local person write such a letter under his or her signature will give local credibility to the letter while controlling its content.

- Submit an article to a newspaper's **OP-ED page**. Small town newspaper editors are always in need of well-written copy on matters of community interest, and this gives you the space (usually around 500 words) and the credibility to make your case. Even major newspapers print unsolicited OP-ED pieces, although the editors of these newspapers can be much more selective as they may receive hundreds or thousands each year.

- Take advantage of editors' needs for copy (and reporters' needs for a story) by issuing press releases. The objective of a press release is to attract the attention of reporters and then provide them with the necessary information to write a good news story. Press releases are especially useful for announcing a newsworthy event, even if that event is an artificial one you have arranged (e.g., a rally, the release of a report, etc.). If your press release is written well, a reporter may even base a story entirely on it. Indeed, small town newspapers may simply print a well-written press release word-for-word as a story.

- Write a press release like a news story, with the "who, what, where, when, and why" of it clearly stated in the first brief paragraph. Keep it clear and to the point (a good press release is usually only one page long), with as little editorial opinion as possible. Send, fax, or deliver a copy of your release to every newspaper, radio, and television station in the targeted areas, as well as to every other reporter, columnist, and commentator who may have an interest. You can get a list of the Statehouse press corps from the **Statehouse pressroom**. The *Illinois Blue Book* also lists all of the TV, radio, and press outlets in the state. Copies of the release may be dropped off in the Statehouse pressroom. If you are going to be at the Statehouse regularly, cultivate contacts in the pressroom, especially with reporters from your home area.

- Press conferences can also be used to attract media coverage and to try to influence its content. Press conferences, even more so than press releases, should be done for hard news only. You will lose credibility with the press quickly if you call a press conference but don't have much to offer. Reserve press conferences for special occasions, such as when a major development has occurred, when someone needs to be questioned by the press, or when the essence of the story cannot be conveyed without one. A press conference should be held in a place and at a time that is as convenient for the media as possible. (There is sometimes a tradeoff between holding a press conference in a convenient place and one with a good visual for TV—such as having a press conference promoting fire safety legislation in front of a burned out building.) Don't expect the Statehouse press corps to show up for a spur-of-the-moment press conference in Macomb on a legislative session day. Send notices a week in advance to all the reporters you would like to attend and then again the day before the event. Call to remind those reporters you especially want to be there.

- Many radio and television stations have local talk and interview shows dealing with public affairs and public policy issues. Identify an articulate and prominent spokesperson for your position (perhaps yourself or a leader of your group) and arrange for him or her to appear on these programs in the targeted areas. Local public affairs programs rarely involve tough or embarrassing questions (although you should watch or listen to a program beforehand), and you can often control the content and tone of the discussion. Indeed, the host will likely ask the guest before the interview what questions he or she would like to be asked. Prepare for questions in advance and promote a lively discussion.
- Work to influence the editorial position

of media outlets in the districts you target by writing to newspaper editors and columnists and radio and television station managers. Offer to meet with them to discuss your position. If possible, bring along a couple of prominent local group members to these meetings. Legislators are particularly sensitive to the editorial opinions of their local media, so while this approach may be time consuming, it can be very effective.

- If a radio or television station takes an editorial position you disagree with, ask for the opportunity to respond. Stations that broadcast editorials will often air opposing viewpoints through editorial replies. However, for commercial reasons, fewer broadcast media take editorial positions today

Taxpayers' Federation of Illinois
300 West Edwards Street • Suite 201 • Springfield, Illinois 62704
217/ 522-6818 • fax 217/ 522-6823

FOR IMMEDIATE RELEASE
June 29, 2000

CONTACT: Tim Bramlet or
Steve Sandstrom, 217 / 522-6818

Taxpayers' Federation supports temporary suspension of sales tax on motor fuel

SPRINGFIELD—The Taxpayers' Federation of Illinois supports the initiative now pending before a special session of the Illinois General Assembly to suspend the state's portion of the sales tax on motor fuel for six months, beginning July 1. The current high prices of retail motor fuel has obviously motivated the action to be taken by the legislature, but it also affords Illinois policymakers the opportunity to examine the impact of such a move on a temporary basis.

"Our only concern with permanent removal of the sales tax on gasoline was its impact on the state's financial picture," said Taxpayers' Federation President Tim Bramlet. "With a six-month window, and a relatively minor impact on the budget, we can make a more educated decision for the future regarding a significant tax policy issue."

Illinois is one of only two Midwestern states that impose the sales tax on motor fuel, creating a tax policy situation that clearly affects the free market. (Indiana, the only other neighboring state to impose the sales tax, suspended it on June 20.) When large industrial or commercial users of motor fuel, as well as many individual motorists, make their purchases, they clearly avoid doing so in Illinois due to the cost differential of the additional tax. Income from additional non-motor fuel purchases from petroleum marketers is also lost.

Unlike other tangible products to which the Illinois sales tax applies, the sales tax on motor fuel imposes a 'tax on a tax.' The Illinois occupation and use tax (sales tax) on motor fuel is imposed upon the base price—plus the federal excise tax of just over 18 cents per gallon. "Forcing Illinois consumers to pay a state tax based partially on an already-imposed federal tax is clearly unfair policy," Bramlet said.

The best tax structure a state can employ is one that is as neutral as possible toward market decisions. Illinois' sales tax on motor fuel violates that principle. It is the additional sales tax on top of the motor fuel tax that results in Illinois having the highest total gasoline taxes in the Midwest.

This six-month window provides the opportunity to examine the impact of such a change and will provide data to guide a later decision over whether making the suspension permanent is both economically productive and fiscally prudent.

– 30 –

A press release should be written like a brief newspaper article, dated, and include contact information.

than previously.

- Check out the local access cable television channels in the districts you target. There are often public affairs forums and talk shows you can participate in, if pre-arranged. While these shows often have very small audiences, they can sometimes be influential because community and opinion leaders may be among the few that do watch. Ask around in the areas you target to see if there are any such programs of importance. Of course, always watch any program before you get involved with it. There are plenty of wacky cable access shows that you will want to avoid.

- Make sure that your position is well represented on all local call-in radio programs. If possible, have group members monitor these in your target areas. Your members should at least respond to the opposition voiced on these shows. A more pro-active approach is to raise your issue and express your opinion purposefully on one or more installments of these shows at important times in the legislative session. One such time is during breaks in the session when legislators are in their home districts. Many legislators keep in touch with their districts by monitoring local radio talk shows.

Using the media can have risks as well as benefits. Sometimes, the media will take the opposing view, and your efforts will only raise the issue in their consciousness, perhaps leading to greater prominence on their editorial pages. If you and your group present extreme positions or make wild claims, you risk losing credibility and being portrayed as crackpots in the media. Your efforts may even draw out latent opposition from other groups or the general public.

Thus, it is vital to have accurate information and to make sure that both you and others representing your group present yourselves as serious, professional, and

A state senator and advocates for a public aquarium hold a press conference.

reasonable citizens. Finally, understand that when working with the media there is always the danger of your message being misrepresented or distorted. In fact, to some degree, this will always happen because the media are expected to interpret from your intentions and message. To minimize this problem, keep your message simple and consistent, and deliver it clearly and repeatedly. Using as many controlled media encounters as possible (e.g., press releases, letters to the editor, OP-ED articles, friendly radio and TV talk shows, etc.) will also help.

Media coverage is only a tool for helping a lobbyist achieve the goals of access and influence. It is not an end in itself. Many persons have waged successful media campaigns, only to have their bills fail in the General Assembly because they didn't take advantage of the opportunities the media campaign provided them. A strong media campaign helps get legislators and others to listen to you. In conjunction with other lobbying tools, it can be effective in helping you pursue your policy goals.

Working with Legislative Staff

Some lobbyists misunderstand the significant role of legislative staff in the Illinois Statehouse and therefore ignore them. This can severely hobble their lobbying efforts, because legislative staff have a critical, if sometimes quiet and subtle, impact on lawmaking. At best, lobbyists who ignore the staff lose out on an opportunity to advance their policy goals. At worst, lobbyists who insult or disrespect staff can find their own influence in the process severely curtailed.

Legislative staff work for the Democratic and Republican leadership in both the Senate and the House. Aside from the

Legislative support agencies

Ten non-partisan and bipartisan legislative agencies provide various research and support services for members of the Illinois General Assembly. These support agencies are:

- Legislative Research Unit
- Legislative Reference Bureau
- Economic and Fiscal Commission
- Intergovernmental Cooperation Commission
- Joint Committee on Administrative Rules
- Legislative Audit Commission
- Legislative Information System
- Legislative Printing Unit
- Space Needs Commission
- Pensions Laws Commission

staff who work for the 10 bipartisan and non-partisan legislative support agencies, almost all professional staff at the Statehouse work for one of the four caucuses. Unlike many other state legislatures and the U.S. Congress, there are very few professional staff controlled by rank-and-file legislators. Typically, at least one staff member for each party is assigned to each standing committee or subject area.

A professional staff member for each party prepares an analysis for each bill that comes before a committee, and this analysis can affect legislators' opinions and actions significantly. Legislators face thousands of decisions on a wide range of issues, and they need help understanding them. Staff analyses are an important way that information regarding bills is distilled for legislative consumption. In fact, legislators cast many of their votes based solely on their party's positions, as reflected in these staff analyses. This is particularly true for quiet, minor bills, which often are the ones that lobbyists and groups advocate. Perhaps the only information a legislator has on such a bill is in the staff analysis. Therefore, it is vital that the information in the staff analyses is accurate and presents your position in the best possible light.

Given the pivotal role of the partisan staff's bill analyses in legislative decision-making, an effective lobbyist works to influence their content and tone. Lobbying staff is in some respects like lobbying legislators. You should treat them with respect and work to help them understand your position. There is a good deal of staff turnover in the Illinois state legislature due to the very hard work they do and the modest pay they receive. Before the legislative session begins, identify the staff members of both parties for the Senate and House who deal with the issues of concern to you and your group. Discuss your legislative agenda for the upcoming session with them, and provide background information as appropriate. Building a sense of trust and respect between yourself and these staff members will go a long way toward facilitating access to them in the hectic and crucial days of the legislative session.

Staff appreciate receiving credible, factual information from reliable sources. Due to limited time and resources during the legislative session, staff sometimes incorporate much or all of a trustworthy lobbyist's Fact Sheet directly into their analyses. Each bill analysis is completed before the bill is heard in committee, so you must contact the relevant staff about a bill immediately upon its introduction. Ask if staff members know of any opposition to the bill, but keep in mind that they may not be forthcoming with this information. Keep in touch with staff throughout the legislative process as they are a great source of information, particularly regarding new developments (both positive and negative) regarding the bill. Senior staff members can be an excellent source of institutional history and procedural information about an issue. In some circumstances, staff may even help you develop a strategy for approaching their members and ultimately passing the legislation. Sometimes staff are asked to help draft bills and amendments for legislators, and it can help your cause to provide assistance in this process, if

Legislative staff perform a crucial role in the legislative process identifying and interpreting policy information for lawmakers.

requested. Do not lobby staff members of the second chamber before the first chamber has passed your bill, as it may be a waste of their time. The committee staff for both parties generally discuss bills prior to committee hearings, so it is important to be fair and equitable in your treatment of both staffs.

committee members as you can before the hearing will allow you to assess the bill's likelihood of passage and to identify the types of changes that might be required to get it favorably (or unfavorably) reported out of the committee. For example, if a committee member has a suggestion that will make the bill more acceptable,

Committee Strategy

In Chapters 3 and 4, we discussed some basic facts about committee procedures. To use this information most effectively in your lobbying efforts, you must begin your work long before the committee meets. As with most other aspects of lobbying, only the proper preparation for your committee work will lead to lobbying success.

As far as possible in advance of a bill's committee hearing, contact the bill sponsor (if you are planning favorable testimony) or an identifiable opponent (if you are planning to testify against the bill), offer your help, and discuss your resources and position. The bill sponsor may ask you to do some legwork on the bill. If so, do your best to respond positively to the request. This is an opportunity to develop access to and credibility with a legislator who works in your policy area and who may help your lobbying efforts on this bill and in the future. Your legwork may include contacting other members of the committee to find out their positions on the bill, to present your position, and to respond to any problems they may have with the bill. This is the kind of action an effective lobbyist would take anyway.

Discussing the bill with as many

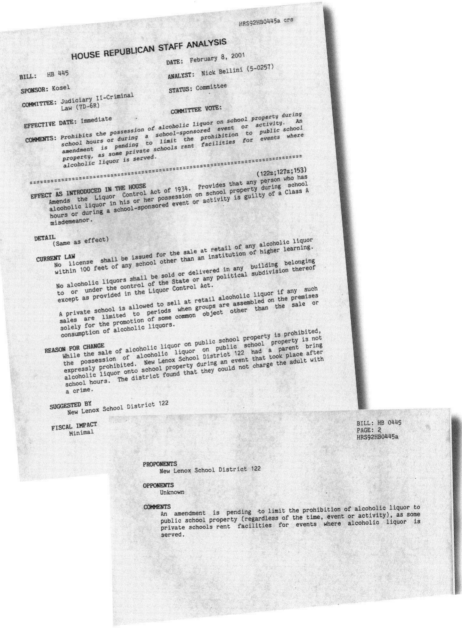

Since legislators are busy and they need to make decisions on so many different bills, they often rely on staff analyses. Generally, staff analyses summarize a bill and include the current law, the intention of the sponsor, its fiscal impact, and any opposition and support. Each party usually has its own staff analysis of each bill assigned to committee.

draft such an amendment before you testify and have the sponsor ready to amend it to the bill if that legislator's vote becomes necessary. Furthermore, by discussing the bill with committee members, you will learn their concerns and what additional information is needed to allay them. Use this information to craft your testimony, addressing these concerns and providing as many of the needed facts as possible.

Your committee legwork might also include conducting a head count to determine how many committee members are in favor of and opposed to the bill. Such information is important for planning lobbying strategy and developing testimony. For example, it allows the sponsor to know when to call the bill for a hearing. Your legwork may also include finding good witnesses who can testify about the bill from experience. Legwork is the time-consuming, nitty-gritty work that needs to be done to ensure that all foreseeable problems are addressed and all potential advantages are seized before your bill comes up for a committee hearing. Don't expect a legislator or legislative staff to do this work for you. Generally, the issue means more to you than it does to them. Be aggressive and make sure the job gets done right.

To avoid wasted effort and potentially damaging mistakes, keep in frequent contact with the lead legislator on your side of the bill (either the sponsor or the main opponent) while preparing for committee action. For instance, a committee member may ask you for some commitment or favor from the sponsor in return for his or her favorable vote on the bill. Report such a request to the sponsor immediately to move the discussion along. Never commit the sponsor unless you have his or her explicit approval to do so. As we discussed in Chapter 4, keeping your sponsor informed is one of your most important responsibilities.

Legislative Party Leadership

In the Illinois General Assembly, political party is the most important organizing principle, and power is concentrated to a large degree in the hands of the chambers' party leaders, or "the Four Tops"—the president and minority leader of the Senate, and the speaker and minority leader of the House. In fact, the Illinois General Assembly is dominated by these party leaders to a far greater extent than are most other state legislatures.

The party leadership plays a major role in organizing the legislature, conducting its business, and stimulating the forces behind the legislative process. You can lobby for leadership support of your bill through your sponsor, the leaders' political allies, legislative staff, and the media. If you decide to seek leadership support, do so early in the process before they have taken a public position against the bill. Leadership support not only lends prestige and credibility to your position, it also provides your bill with extra votes and visibility. Party leaders can also help steer your bill in the direction that will most likely lead to its success.

On the other hand, leadership support and attention for your bill may take its fate out of your hands in ways that you and your group may not like. Active leadership work on a bill heightens the attention that the media and other legislators give to it. If the bill is seen as partisan, you may gain some votes and lose others. Leadership may see the bill as a minor component of its overall legislative strategy, modifying it in ways you may not like or killing it in exchange for some advantage elsewhere. Your best bet is to use leadership support cautiously. Be specific about your requests and ask for favors only when absolutely necessary to keep the bill moving and alive. Sometimes the best lobbying strategy is not to seek leadership support (without gaining their enmity), and argue that the bill does very little and is a bipartisan solution that any legislator can vote for with no drawbacks.

In considering the role of party and party leadership in your lobbying strategy, note that the majority party leadership has much more power in a chamber than the minority party leadership. If the majority party leadership wants to expend the political capital necessary to rally their own party members, they can win any vote (except, perhaps, those that require a super-majority). They also control many of the procedural aspects of the process, such as committee assignments of bills and floor scheduling. A sponsor from the majority party may get better treatment for his or her bill than one from the

minority party (although this is not always the case). A further complication is that the chambers may have different majority parties, a situation know as **split control** that has been common in recent Illinois General Assemblies. Under split control of the legislature, it may be advantageous to have chief sponsors in the different chambers from different parties, so that each is from the majority in his or her respective chamber. This may be difficult on some issues, often requiring negotiation and compromise.

Legislative Coalitions

The internal politics of each chamber plays an important role in the success or failure of any bill. **Legislative coalitions**, that is, groups of legislators who have similar interests and work together to

Split control: When one party holds a majority in one chamber of the legislature and another party holds the majority in the other chamber. Split control can also refer to the situation where the governor is of a different party than at least one of the chambers' majority.

Legislative coalition: A group of legislators who share a common legislative interest and pursue it together. Coalitions may be formal or informal, long-term or temporary. Generally, such coalitions have interest groups and lobbyists working with them, again, either long-term or temporarily.

The "Four Tops" pose with leaders of a veterans' organization.

pursue these interests, are an important part of these internal politics. These coalitions may be formally organized with a name, officers, and meetings (e.g., the Legislative Black Caucus), or they may be informal (e.g., downstate Democrats). They may endure session after session, or they may form for only one bill. As a lobbyist, you must be aware of the coalitions that work in your policy area, as well as those that may arise through your, or your opposition's, instigation. Thus, you must work to gain the support not only of individual legislators, but also of those legislators who formally or informally represent these coalitions in each chamber. Coalition support can be a real time-saver, allowing you to gain the immediate support of a number of legislators.

The most obvious and enduring cleavages in the Illinois state legislature and in Illinois politics are defined by party and geography— Chicago (dominated by Democrats), the collar counties/Chicago suburbs (dominated by Republicans), downstate Democrats, and downstate Republicans. The memberships of the more formal Legislative Black Caucus, Latino Caucus, and Conference of Women Legislators (CoWL) can cross party lines acting on selected issues based on their common values and interests. Ongoing informal coalitions also develop around some perennial policy issues (e.g., education, abortion, the Chicago-area Regional Transit Authority, agriculture, coal mining). These coalitions often extend across party lines. Work with your sponsor to identify the various coalitions that might be interested in your bill and the key legislators who represent them. If possible, gain the support of these informal coalition leaders early in the process, even before the parties take positions on the bill.

Building Your Own Coalition

Effective lobbyists are always on the lookout for allies. There probably are many groups whose interests line up regularly with your interests, as well as groups whose interests line up regularly in opposition. Identify those groups, lobbyists, and legislators who frequently support your position on bills and who introduce bills that you favor. These are your natural allies. Developing a working relationship with these people will enhance your power and influence in the legislative process and improve the prospects of your bills passing into law. Some of these allies may already be informed about and taking an active interest in your bills. Others will need to be convinced of their stake in the outcome. This sort of informal coalition of lobbyists, groups, and legislators with common interests can be very useful in every phase of the legislative process.

Developing a coalition, even if it is an ad hoc coalition working together for only one bill, increases your power base for many reasons. First, two (or more) heads can be better than one. Your coalition partners will bring more policy and political information to the table, offer more ideas for policy arguments and political angles, and have more connections with individual legislators than you do by yourself. But what is often more important, a coalition shows legislators that a number of interests have worked through a policy problem to formulate a compromise solution. The larger and more diverse your coalition is, the greater this effect. But, of course, the larger and more diverse your coalition, the harder it is to bring everyone together. Legislators know this, which is why a diverse coalition is so impressive. Legislators and legislative leaders like to avoid conflict. They prefer to ratify a compromise worked out elsewhere.

If you represent a small, inexperienced, local, or in some other way less-than-powerful group, it is particularly important to develop coalitions with more powerful interests. Such an alliance will give you access to people and places that would otherwise be closed to you. Furthermore, your relationships with other groups will be valuable for future lobbying activities. In short, lobby other lobbyists for cooperation. The future payoff can be large, even if your efforts aren't immediately successful.

In addition to ad hoc coalitions formed to promote or defeat particular bills, ongoing coalitions may develop in a policy area, such as the Illinois Statewide School Management Alliance, the Illinois Safe Kids Coalition, and the Illinois Coalition of Electric Utilities Companies. The more often these informal coalitions are active, the closer their members are identified with one another, both among themselves and by those outside the coalition. Bills that affect the common interests of members stimulate such a coalition into legislative action. Telephone networks, monthly or weekly strategy meetings before and during a legislative session, and simple conversations in and around the Statehouse can solidify these coalitions and help mobilize them when needed.

Tips on Working with Coalitions

Working with coalitions offers distinct advantages to lobbyists and interest groups, but it is often a difficult undertaking. It is much easier to direct your own efforts— a dictatorship is more efficient than a democracy! You have to weigh the potential benefits of coalition activity against the extra effort and energy demanded of you to see whether it is the right approach to pursue on a given bill. Here are a few tips to help the coalition process go more smoothly:

- Understand that your coalition partners may be fair-weather friends who may turn against you on the next bill. Don't take this personally—they are just looking out for their own best interests. That's just politics. Think of an ad hoc coalition as a one-time-only lobbying tactic to accomplish a specific and immediate goal, such as passing a bill out of committee. Don't count on your allies for long-term support until you have long-term experience with them.
- Individual ego needs and personal agendas may sometimes interfere with effective decision-making and lobbying in an interest group coalition. A coalition's most important asset is its

The Legislative Black Caucus pursues its common interests, as do other legislative coalitions.

unity of purpose. For a coalition to be effective, these internal problems must be suppressed to create the public impression of coalition unity, at least until the coalition's goal is achieved.

- In face-to-face lobbying, vary the coalition's spokesperson according to which allied group has the most clout with the legislator(s) being lobbied. But don't assign any duties to someone who represents an inappropriate group, who may make ill-advised compromises, or who may in some other way bring disrepute to the coalition.

- Avoid the temptation for the coalition to become active on such a wide range of issues that it overextends its resources, undermines its unity of purpose, and loses its influence with legislators. Keep focused on clear and specific goals. Save your political strength for the big battles rather than diffusing it on every issue that comes along.

Using Litigation in Lobbying

Legislation and litigation are sometimes seen as alternative approaches to solving a policy problem, but they can also be used together to good effect. A successful lawsuit may sometimes force your opposition to change its views, but even just the credible threat of litigation can be a potent lobbying weapon. You may be able to convince your opponents that the unknown and potentially large cost of litigation could surpass the cost of supporting your position. Thus, litigation may encourage the opposition to seek a compromise. When trying to defeat a bill, a related strategy is to argue that the legislation is unconstitutional and will be struck down by the courts. By coordinating your litigation and legislative strategies, you may enhance your chances of succeeding in either arena.

On the other hand, litigation-based strategies have their drawbacks. Litigation, or the threat of it, allows your opponents to use the argument that the legislature should wait on the issue until the courts have made a decision. This effect also works in reverse; a court might be convinced to postpone action on a suit until the legislature has acted. And, of course, courts can rule against you. Therefore, like other strategies, the

Illinois's three principal political regions are Chicago, the Collar Counties (the suburban counties surrounding Chicago), and Downstate (the rest of the state). These regions are often distinct in their politics, economics, demographics, and policy interests.

SOURCE: Reprinted from ILLINOIS POLITICS AND GOVERNMENT: THE EXPANDING FRONTIER by Samuel K. Gove and James D. Nowlan by permission of the University of Nebraska Press. © 1996 by the University of Nebraska Press.

litigation strategy has risks that must be weighed carefully against the potential benefits.

Federal Policy in State-Level Lobbying

In many policy areas, both the federal and state governments have legal authority. Whenever this is the case, consider using arguments about federal policy in your state-level lobbying efforts. Programs that you favor might be eligible for federal funding. Find out if this is true before the legislative session, and make sure your bill is written to take advantage of this opportunity. Most importantly, highlight the availability of federal funding in your lobbying arguments. Perhaps the most common argument made in opposition to legislation is that it costs too much. The availability of federal funding undercuts this argument. From the state's point of view, federal money is free money (or cheap money, for programs with matching federal funds) and thus reduces the cost of an eligible program.

Some legislation can be helped or hurt by the proper interpretation of federal law. A written interpretation from the federal agency involved is the best evidence here. Sometimes, a carefully placed telephone call from a state legislator can get this accomplished. (Of course, federal officials are not nearly as responsive to state legislators as are state officials. A call from a congressperson might get better results.) When you are trying to kill a bill, potential conflicts with federal law can be used to raise doubts for undecided legislators.

But don't be surprised if legislators don't respond to the argument that a bill you oppose violates federal law. In fact, many otherwise rational legislators become angry and stubborn in the face of pressure from the "Feds." They will not tolerate federal meddling in state affairs! Often, the only way the federal government can get the Illinois General Assembly (or any other state legislature) to go along with its programs is to entice it with federal dollars. ❑

Chapter **6**
Administrative Rulemaking—
Lobbying State Agencies

The legislature often gives state administrative agencies broad authority and discretion to implement laws. State agencies adopt and **promulgate** rules and regulations that have the force of law in carrying out a statute. Of course, a state agency cannot change a statute, and its rules must conform to legislative intent. However, statutory language is often vague, leaving considerable leeway to the agency in determining specific requirements. Thus, administrative rules are often as important as the statute itself in the impact they have on people and businesses in the state. Remember, the devil is in the details!

Although administrative rules are extremely important, there is often surprisingly little public involvement in their development. Agency staffers draft many rules with little or no public input. This need not be the case. Administrative agency officials, like members of the legislature, can and should be lobbied to shape the actions of state government to fit the needs of its citizens. The development of rules and regulations should be subject to negotiation and compromise among interested parties, within the boundaries of the underlying statute. Many of the same tools used in legislative lobbying are appropriate for agency lobbying. One important difference is that the lobbyist must be familiar with the powers and the politics of the specific agency involved.

The **Illinois Administrative Procedure Act** (IAPA) (5 ILCS 100) is the statute that governs administrative rulemaking and outlines the process an agency must follow whenever it adopts a policy that affects anyone outside the agency, such as the public or another agency. While the IAPA encompasses all three branches of government in its definition of an "agency," most rulemaking is conducted by administrative agencies in the executive branch, that is, those agencies under the direction of the **constitutional officers** (the governor, lieutenant governor, secretary of state, attorney general, treasurer, and comptroller).

State agencies, boards, and commissions bring their policy agendas to the General Assembly for approval through the creation of statutory authority for a program or policy and by seeking funding for their programs and policies through the appropriations process. Programs and policies can also be assigned to an administrative agency through legislative

Promulgate: To publish and make widely known. When administrative agencies make rules, they promulgate them by publishing them in the *Illinois Administrative Code*.

Illinois Administrative Procedure Act: The statute (5 ILCS 100) that governs administrative rulemaking and outlines the process an agency must follow whenever it adopts a policy that affects anyone outside the agency, such as the public or another agency.

Constitutional officers: Elected executive branch officers with statewide jurisdiction that are explicitly defined in the Illinois Constitution— the governor, lieutenant governor, secretary of state, attorney general, treasurer, and comptroller.

First Notice: The phase of administrative rulemaking that is primarily focused on public input and conducted by the agency itself.

Second Notice: The phase of administrative rulemaking that is primarily focused on legislative review of a rulemaking and conducted by the General Assembly's Joint Committee on Administrative Rules (JCAR).

Joint Committee on Administrative Rules (JCAR): A bipartisan oversight committee of the General Assembly created to ensure that the legislature is informed about how laws are implemented through agency rulemaking, to facilitate public understanding of rules and regulations, and to ensure that agency rules are adequate, appropriate, and in compliance with legislative intent. The committee is composed of 12 legislators appointed by the party leaders for two-year terms, with equal representation of Democrats and Republicans and senators and representatives. Support services are provided to the committee by a staff of approximately 25 persons.

Notice of Proposed Rulemaking: The official notice of a proposed rulemaking that is published along with the proposed rule text and notifies the public of the form (written, oral, public hearing, etc.) in which and to whom comments may be submitted to the agency.

initiative. Citizens can support or oppose these proposed policies as they move through the legislative process. Similarly, the IAPA provides an opportunity for citizen input when agencies pursue their policy agendas through administrative rulemaking.

The Origin of Rules

Administrative rules promulgated by state agencies originate from a range of sources for a variety of reasons. Legislation enacted by the General Assembly often requires an agency to adopt rules to implement it in a "timely and expeditious manner." Federal policies, court decisions, and collective bargaining agreements may require that administrative rules be adopted. Furthermore, under Section 5-145 of the IAPA, any person may simply request the adoption, amendment, or repeal of a rule. If rulemaking is not initiated within 30 days of such a request, the request is considered denied.

The Rulemaking Process

The IAPA creates a two-step process for rule adoption or amendment, with the opportunity for public input at both steps. The two steps are referred to as **First Notice**, which is primarily focused on public input and conducted by the agency itself, and **Second Notice**, which is primarily

Types of rules

Regular rules: Administrative rules developed and promulgated through the regular process.

Emergency rules: Rules developed under emergency conditions, which for purposes of the IAPA are defined as "the existence of any situation that any agency finds reasonably constitutes a threat to the public interest, safety, or welfare."

Peremptory rules: Rules required by federal law, federal rules and regulations, an order of a court, or a collective bargaining agreement.

Required rules: Rules that agencies are required by the IAPA to maintain.

focused on legislative review of a rulemaking and conducted by the General Assembly's **Joint Committee on Administrative Rules (JCAR)**.

First Notice begins when an agency files a rulemaking proposal with the Secretary of State's Index Department for publication in the weekly *Illinois Register*. For at least 45 days after that publication, anyone may submit data, opinions, arguments, and comments to the proposing agency. The **Notice of Proposed Rulemaking**, published along with the proposed rule text, notifies the public of the form (written, oral, public hearing, etc.) in which and to whom comments may be submitted to the agency. A separate public hearing notice may also be published later by the agency.

One or more public hearings on the proposed rulemaking may be held during First Notice, if either 1) the agency voluntarily schedules a hearing, or 2) the agency receives a request for a public hearing within the first 14 days after publication of the Notice of Proposed Rulemaking from at least 25 persons, an association representing at least 100 persons, the governor, JCAR, or an affected unit of local government.

Anytime after the conclusion of the 45-day First Notice period, the agency can submit the proposed rule, as modified in response to public comment, to JCAR, thereby beginning the Second Notice period. The only limitation on how long an agency can wait to make its Second

Notice submission is that JCAR must be allowed at least a 45-day Second Notice period before the rulemaking's expiration, which is one year after the date of First Notice publication.

In addition to this regular rulemaking process, the IAPA also provides three ways to expedite rulemaking when necessary:

- **Emergency rules** may be promulgated to be effective immediately upon filing with the secretary of state or on a stated date within 10 days after filing. A Notice of Emergency Rulemaking, which includes the agency's reasons for not using the regular process and the text of the emergency rule, are then published in the *Illinois Register*. An emergency rule is effective for a maximum of 150 days, during which time either the situation leading to the rule is resolved or a companion rulemaking is adopted through the regular rulemaking procedures. An emergency rule cannot be continued beyond the 150 days through adoption of a subsequent emergency rule with the same provision.

- **Peremptory rules** are those required as a result of federal law, federal rules and regulations, an order of a court, or a collective bargaining agreement. The federal law or rule, court order, or collective bargaining agreement leaves the agency no discretion on the content of the rule, hence rendering public and JCAR comments moot. Peremptory rules are effective immediately upon filing with the secretary of state, or at a date required or authorized by the relevant federal law or rules, court order, or collective bargaining agreement. A Notice of Peremptory Rulemaking must be published in the *Illinois Register* within 30 days after the action that necessitated the rulemaking.

- **Required rules** are those rules that agencies are required by the IAPA to maintain. They can be adopted unilaterally by the agency filing them with the secretary of state. These include organizational charts, agency address information, Freedom of Information Act procedures, hearing officer qualifications, and similar housekeeping measures.

In addition to the promulgation of specific and binding rules, each agency

The *Illinois Register* is the official state publication designed to keep the public informed of administrative rulemaking activity. It is published every Friday by the Secretary of State's Index Department and contains First Notice publication of rulemaking proposals, JCAR actions, notices of final adoption of rulemakings, Regulatory Agendas (in January and July), and Executive Orders and Proclamations. Periodically, it also includes indices to the current and previous issues. An annual subscription to the *Illinois Register* can be purchased from the Secretary of State's Index Department.

Declaratory ruling: An advisory opinion issued by an agency on the applicability or meaning of any statute, rule, or order pertaining to that agency. A declaratory ruling may also determine whether compliance with a federal rule will be accepted as compliance with an Illinois rule.

Regulatory Agenda: A list of rules under consideration for revision or new rules drafted to implement new programs but not yet in First Notice. Agencies must publish their Regulatory Agenda in the *Illinois Register* twice a year, by January 1 and July 1.

may (at its discretion) provide for the filing and disposition of requests for **declaratory rulings**. These are advisory opinions issued by an agency on the applicability or meaning of a statute, rule, or order. Each agency must also submit a **Regulatory Agenda** for publication in the *Illinois Register* by January 1 and July 1 each year for the purpose of eliciting public comments regarding any rule under consideration but for which First Notice has not yet been published.

Reference materials identified in a proposed rulemaking are available from the agency upon request for inspection and copying at cost.

Recording Rules

The Secretary of State's Index Department keeps open to public inspection a permanent file of all agency rules. Each agency must also keep a copy of its own rules available for public inspection, along with materials incorporated into the rule by reference, all final orders, decisions, and opinions, except those deemed confidential by statute or that deal with trade secrets.

The ***Illinois Administrative Code*** is the compilation of all agency rules, published by the secretary of state. Updated quarterly, the *Illinois Administrative Code* is available on CD-ROM at an annual subscription rate. For more information on obtaining subscriptions to the *Illinois Administrative Code,* call (217) 782-7015 and the *Illinois Register*, call (217) 782-0650 or visit the Secretary of State's Index Department's Web site at: http://www.cyberdriveillinois.com/departments/index/dept_index.html.

Inquiries about rules or ordering the text of a specific part of a rule should be directed to:

Illinois Administrative Code: A compilation of all agency rules published by the Secretary of State's Index Department. The *Code* is maintained electronically by JCAR and LIS.

Secretary of State
Index Department
Administrative Code Division
111 E. Monroe Street
Springfield, IL 62756
Telephone: (217) 785-7538

Rules and parts of rules may also be ordered online. The *Illinois Administrative Code* and the *Illinois Register* are also available online through the General Assembly's Legislative Information Service (LIS) and several contractual vendors, including Westlaw, Lexis-Nexis, and Law Office Information Services.

Joint Committee on Administrative Rules

The Joint Committee on Administrative Rules (JCAR) is a bipartisan legislative agency created to monitor the compliance of agencies with the requirements of the IAPA (25 ILCS 130/2-1 [Statutory Authority] and 5 ILCS 100/5-90 through 5-140 [Description and Responsibilities]). Composed of 12 legislators representing both chambers and parties equally and appointed by the legislative leadership, JCAR:

- Reviews the statutory authority for each proposed administrative rule, along with other criteria, such as agency use of discretion and economic impact;
- Maintains a review program to study the impact of legislative changes, court rulings, and administrative action on agency rules and rulemaking;
- Suggests rulemaking to an agency when, in the course of its review, JCAR determines the agency's rules are

incomplete, inconsistent, or otherwise deficient.

JCAR employs a staff of about 25 to assist in reviewing administrative rules and to assure that the requirements and procedures outlined in the IAPA have been followed throughout the rulemaking process. JCAR has the authority to examine any proposed or adopted rule, make recommendations, raise objections, temporarily delay implementation, and, as a last resort, request the assistance of the General Assembly as a whole in permanently prohibiting or suspending a rulemaking.

While its role in the rulemaking process is officially just an advisory one, in practice, JCAR is active and influential in the legislative oversight of agency rulemaking. Agencies, groups, the General Assembly, and JCAR members themselves take their role in the process very seriously.

Public Comment to JCAR

The First Notice period is officially designated as the time for public input on rulemaking, and Second Notice is the legislative review period. But as a part of the legislative review, JCAR accepts public comment on a rulemaking at any time prior to its consideration at a monthly JCAR meeting. You can contact JCAR if an agency has not been responsive to your comments or if you missed the First Notice public comment period. Complaints about existing rules and suggestions for change should be submitted to the agency first, but you may then forward them to JCAR for consideration. JCAR has the authority to open an investigation into an existing rule at any time.

As part of Second Notice, JCAR receives a copy or summary of all the public comments the agency received during the First Notice period. If JCAR believes that

JCAR offices are located in Room 700 Stratton Building.

the agency did not give due consideration to a comment from the public, it can continue to explore that issue with the agency during its Second Notice review.

To be more effective in relating your concerns to JCAR, identify the JCAR staffperson responsible for handling the administrative rulemaking or agency of interest to you and contact him or her directly with your comments. If you are unable to identify a specific staffperson, address your comments to:

Executive Director
Joint Committee on
    Administrative Rules
700 Stratton Building
Springfield, IL 62706
Telephone: (217) 785-2254
Email: JCAR@legis.state.il.us

In addition to discussing your position and arguments with the relevant JCAR staffperson, you should also make your case directly to the legislative members of JCAR. This is especially important because JCAR only takes oral testimony from the agency proposing the rulemaking. Thus, it is vital to speak to JCAR members personally, especially if your position on a rulemaking is different than that of the proposing agency. JCAR members need and want to know how a proposal will affect people and businesses in the state. Your personal arguments in this regard, the written materials you submit, and the briefing you give JCAR staff will enhance your chances of successfully achieving your policy goals.

JCAR Actions

In the regular rulemaking process, as a result of its review in the Second Notice period, JCAR may take one of several actions regarding the proposed rulemaking:

- **Certificate of No Objection.** With this certificate, the agency can adopt and promulgate the rulemaking by filing it with the secretary of state for publication in the *Illinois Register* and *Illinois Administrative Code.*
- **Recommendation (issued along with a Certificate of No Objection).** The agency must respond to the recommendation in writing within 90 days. It can modify or withdraw the rulemaking in response to the recommendation (but note that after going to Second Notice, the agency cannot unilaterally modify or withdraw a rulemaking). However, the agency may also adopt the rulemaking with no changes.
- **Objection.** An agency must respond to an objection in writing within 90 days, but after responding it can proceed to adopt the rulemaking. The agency can modify or withdraw the rulemaking in response to the objection, or it can adopt the rulemaking without changes. JCAR Agreements (i.e., Second Notice changes) still apply. The agency's response goes on the JCAR monthly meeting agenda for further consideration.
- **Filing Prohibition/Suspension.** If JCAR determines that a rulemaking

constitutes a threat to the public interest, safety, or welfare, it can by a three-fifths vote of its members prohibit filing of a proposed rulemaking (or suspend an emergency or peremptory rule). As a result, for a period of 180 days, the proposed rulemaking cannot be accepted for filing by the secretary of state or enforced by the agency, nor can an emergency or peremptory rule that has already been adopted be enforced. A prohibition/suspension lasts for a maximum of 180 days, within which time the JCAR action may be withdrawn if the agency offers satisfactory modifications to the rulemaking. If no modifications or offer to withdraw are forthcoming from the agency in this period, JCAR is to cause a joint resolution to be introduced in the General Assembly through which that body may permanently continue the prohibition/suspension. If the joint resolution is not approved within the 180-day period, the agency may file the proposed rule for adoption, or the suspension is lifted and the emergency or peremptory rulemaking is in effect again.

Advocacy on Administrative Rulemaking

The procedures under the IAPA for adopting and promulgating administrative rules provide significant avenues for a lobbyist to influence state agency policies and procedures.

Monitoring Rulemaking

Just as it is vital to monitor legislation to assure that your interests are not hurt by someone else's actions, a good lobbyist monitors the rulemaking process conscientiously. An important tool for doing this efficiently is **The Flinn Report: Illinois Regulation**, a four- to six-page weekly publication produced by JCAR summarizing the rulemaking activity in that week's *Illinois Register. The Flinn Report* can be a good way to determine whether you want to pursue an issue more thoroughly through the much lengthier *Illinois Register. The Flinn Report* is available free of charge upon request to JCAR or it can be viewed online at the General Assembly Web site: http://www.legis.state.il.us/ commission/jcar/flinn_rpts.html.

Follow the *Flinn Report* or the *Illinois Register* weekly so that you know when a rulemaking that might affect your group's interests is proposed. You should also try to maintain contact with the program or rules staff in agencies that deal with your policy area. In this way, you may be able to review and comment on proposals even before they are filed officially. Also, in January and July, check the Regulatory Agenda published by relevant agencies in the *Illinois Register*.

First Notice Period

During the 45-day First Notice public comment period after a proposed regulation is published in the *Illinois Register*, you should:

- Analyze the proposed regulation carefully. Determine if it implements the statute as you interpret that statute, if it is practical, and if it goes too far or not far enough.
- Consult with your group, fellow lobbyists, local administrators, providers or contractors, consumer organizations, and others who will be affected by the proposed rulemaking.
- Request that the agency hold a public hearing when the proposed rulemaking raises significant, controversial issues affecting your group, especially

if large numbers of people and businesses may be affected. A hearing must be requested in *the first 14 days* of the 45-day First Notice period, so time is of the essence.

- Gather the facts necessary to support your position on how the proposed rulemaking should be adjusted to serve your group better. Specific suggestions for change are usually much more successful than general concerns or complaints.
- Urge all those with a direct or indirect interest in the proposal, and who have the same or similar position as you and your group, to file comments.

The Flinn Report: **Illinois Regulation** is a four- to six-page weekly summary of rulemaking activity in the *Illinois Register*, published by JCAR. *The Flinn Report* is available free of charge upon request to JCAR, or it can be viewed online at the General Assembly Web site: http://www.legis.state.il.us/commission/jcar/flinn_rpts.html.

A good relationship with agency decision-makers helps lobbyists succeed in the rulemaking process.

Provide them with a draft of your own comments.

- Send the agency a clear, concise, and well-researched statement of objections and recommendations for change. Send a copy of these comments to JCAR.
- Identify the JCAR staffperson responsible for the proposed rulemaking.
- Do all of the above promptly. Don't wait until the 44th day of the First Notice period!

Second Notice

At the end of the 45-day First Notice period, the agency reviews all the comments it has received, makes whatever changes to its proposed rulemaking it deems appropriate based on these comments, and then submits the Second Notice to JCAR. The Second Notice includes the revised rule text, a summary of all comments, and an explanation of why these comments were accepted or rejected. By statute, JCAR has up to 45 days to review the rulemaking. However, because JCAR needs to review the

rulemaking at its subsequent monthly meeting, it seldom has the full 45 days. So, again, do not delay in submitting your comments to JCAR. Note that all First and Second Notice written comments are public record and can be viewed upon request.

If your concerns with the rulemaking remain after it is modified by the agency following First Notice, be sure to let JCAR know that the agency's First Notice changes did not resolve your objections. Furthermore, consider and comment on any problems that might have been created for you and your group by the changes made by the agency after First Notice. To determine what changes were made, ask the agency or JCAR staffperson involved. Second Notice changes can also occur, when agreed upon by JCAR and the agency, so keep an eye out for these changes as well.

JCAR is particularly interested in issues such as whether the rulemaking:

- Is within the agency's statutory authority;
- Is consistent with the legislative intent

for the statute;

- Includes sufficient standards for the exercise of discretion by agency personnel to guarantee equal application of the law;
- Creates any undue economic impact on the state or the affected public;
- Has any undue negative impact on small business, small municipalities, or not-for-profit corporations;
- Creates a new state mandate;
- Suggests that the agency may be adhering to "policy not in the rules" (created through policy manuals, internal memos, etc.); and
- Complies with the *Administrative Code* format, is technically well constructed, and is as easy to read as possible.

These are all points to consider about a rulemaking you object to and to highlight in your public comments, as appropriate.

Administrative Advocacy

Access to the administrative arena is just as important as access to the legislature. Get to know the decision-making staff in the administrative agencies that affect you and your group. It is essential that you develop a working relationship with a few persons in those agencies who can alert you when important decisions that could affect your group are about to be made or when budget and policy directives are about to be adopted informally. In particular, get to know these agencies' **legislative liaisons**. Legislative liaisons function as lobbyists for their agencies with the legislature and may well empathize with your policy concerns and

Although they may work hard and conscientiously, agency employees are subject to frequent criticism from the public, the press, and legislators. Consider the negative connotation people often put on the terms "bureaucrat" and "state employee." A little friendliness and a compliment now and then can get you a long way. These people typically are hard-working professionals who deserve praise and respect.

your role in the process.

You can also use the legislature to gain access to administrative agencies. State agencies are generally very sensitive to the concerns and criticisms of members of the legislature. A letter or telephone call from a senator or representative who sits on the standing committee that reviews an agency's programs or an appropriations committee that reviews its annual budget may accomplish what you cannot accomplish alone, even if it is only opening doors to make your case to an agency decision-maker. The annual budget process provides a regular opportunity to raise your policy concerns with an agency. You can strengthen your request for a change in an agency's rules by convincing a legislator to raise the problem with the agency at its budget hearing. Coordinating your legislative and regulatory efforts with litigation, if necessary and when appropriate, may produce such a barrage of activity that even an initially unresponsive agency may come around to your way of thinking.

The bottom line is that administrative agency officials, like members of the legislature, need to be lobbied to ensure that state government policy best meets the needs of your group. Just as in the legislative process, rulemaking is subject to negotiation, compromise, and advocacy. Knowing the players and the process is just as important in rulemaking as it is in lawmaking. Given the specificity and impact of agency rules, rulemaking can be just as crucial to your group's interests as the enactment of a statute. ❏

Legislative liaison: An administrative agency employee who acts as a lobbyist for his or her agency with the legislature.

Chapter **7**
Lobbying and Grassroots Politics

In recent years, more citizens have stopped asking, "*Why* should I get involved in the political process?" Instead, recognizing the importance of a strong voice in the state capitol, citizens are now asking, "*How* can I get involved in the political process most effectively?"

For many, the answer to this question is to join forces with other like-minded citizens and form politically active groups. Taking their cue from business groups, citizens across Illinois are organizing to make their voices heard in the policy-making process. These are groups, like the Alzheimer's Association of Greater Chicagoland, the Jo Daviess/Stephenson 4-Lane 20 Association, and the Pope County Anti-Hunger League, whose members care enough about an issue to spend their time and effort trying to influence public policy. Often, these local groups link up with similar groups in other communities, forming regional or statewide networks.

A network of **grassroots organizations** can supply a lobbyist with a very powerful punch in his or her efforts to influence public policy—a unified constituency that legislators want and need to satisfy. Even a small group can have an impact.

Legislators understand that for every citizen who makes the effort to join an organization or write a letter or make a telephone call, there are many more who agree with that position but just aren't moved enough to act. Plus, since these citizens often do take the time to vote, their opinions matter greatly to elected officials.

> *The legislator's district is where political power resides, and grassroots lobbying puts legislators into contact with constituents who hold that power. It demonstrates vocal and tangible support (or opposition) for a measure. In a grassroots campaign, constituents tell legislators how the measure will affect them, instead of the lobbyist doing it.*
>
> Alan Rosenthal (1993, 155)

Grassroots organization: A group of persons who organize to advocate for public policies that reflect their mutual interests.

What Is a Grassroots Organization?

A grassroots lobbying organization is simply a group of persons who organize to advocate for public policies that reflect

Contract lobbyist: An independent lobbyist who works for a variety of clients and is paid on a contractual basis. A contract lobbyist may make his or her living solely through lobbying, or he or she may also do legal, public relations, or other work. A contract lobbyist may work with a firm or independently, and he or she may only take on certain types of clients.

their mutual interests. Aside from that fundamental description, these groups vary widely in size, structure, membership, activities, and funding. Grassroots groups in Illinois reflect the state's diversity, as effective organizations grow indigenously from their communities.

These groups exist in many forms. Some are highly structured organizations, with officers, elections, bylaws, and dues, holding regular meetings, and publishing newsletters. Others are merely small groups of friends and neighbors meeting around a kitchen table after they put the kids to bed but who know other folks who can be relied on to take part in a telephone, letter-writing, or e-mail campaign when the need arises. Some groups consist of citizens from a specific geographic area and focus on a single issue, such as parents

from a single school district interested in a curriculum issue. Others have chapters around the state and are interested in broader issues at the state level.

There is no single best way to organize a group. An effective grassroots organization is tailored to its particular community and its particular issue. The degree of political sophistication, level of interest, and amount of time people are willing to devote to legislative action will determine how a group is best organized.

What a Grassroots Group Can Do

The strength of a grassroots group comes from its roots—the people who belong to it and those who sympathize with its aims. An effective grassroots organization has members who will act together in the policy-making process at the proper time, as directed by their leaders. This action may be as little as writing a letter or making a telephone call to a legislator, or it may be handing out fliers or testifying at a legislative or administrative hearing. The responsibility for mobilizing these people to act at the proper time falls on the group leaders. These leaders must maintain lists of members and monitor the policy-making process so that they can alert members about what to do and when to do it. Professional lobbyists, often contract lobbyists, may work with group leaders to accomplish these tasks. A grassroots organization may hire such a lobbyist, or more commonly, the group may get guidance from a lobbyist working for allied groups on the same issue.

A citizen group can lobby lawmakers and state executives (including the governor) by letter, telephone, e-mail, petition, or in

WE NEED YOUR VOICE!

day care action council of Illinois

PARENT LOBBY DAY

April 25, 2002
10:30 a.m.
Illinois State Capitol Rotunda Area
2nd Street & Capitol Avenue
Springfield, Illinois

Make your voice heard in Springfield. We need to show legislators how child care affects you and your families. The day will include a rally and opportunity to talk to your legislator.

WHEN CHILD CARE WORKS, ILLINOIS WORKS

For more information, please contact your center staff.

A grassroots group may decide that descending en masse on the Statehouse is a useful way of showing legislators the level of support for its position. These "lobby days" can be fun and useful for maintaining group members' interest in the cause. However, to be effective in policy-making, lobby days must be well planned, well timed, and used to support a long-term and thoughtful lobbying strategy.

person. As long as the group members are volunteers, they do not even need to register as lobbyists. Groups, through their members, also can testify before legislative committees, provide background information to legislators and their staff, organize candidate forums and debates, and publish voting records and information on issues.

Given the unexpected speed with which many legislative matters sometimes move, an **alert network** is usually needed to respond to fast-breaking developments at the Statehouse. An alert network is a list of members that a group leader can count on to contact legislators on short notice. This may take the form of an old-fashioned telephone tree, where a leader calls four members, who each call four other members, and so on, as the message fans out across the group's membership. The modern alternative is an e-mail listserv or a contact list for mass e-mailing. An effective alert network will get at least ten *personal* letters to (or make other contacts with) a targeted official within one week.

Remember, one original, personal, heartfelt letter or telephone call, even a short one, is worth 50 rubber-stamped, identical postcards. Policy-makers understand the difference in commitment required between these two forms of correspondence. It is the difference between real grassroots action and **Astroturf**.

In addition to lobbying, a citizen group may be able to strengthen its voice by actively supporting (or opposing) candidates for political office. Political action of this sort is regulated by law in Illinois, so you need to be careful in making official group campaign contributions and endorsements (see Chapter 8). But, for example, the voluntary work of your group members on a legislator's campaign is unregulated and usually very much welcome. Also, at campaign time (which increasingly is any time of the year), legislators often look for opportunities to get their messages out. An invitation to speak before your group may be beneficial to both of your interests.

Alert network: A list of members that a group leader can count on to contact a policy-maker on short notice.

Astroturf: An expression for artificially generated grass-roots political activity. For example, 50 people at a group meeting signing and sending identical post cards to a state legislator on a bill is Astroturf. Like Astroturf in a baseball stadium, political Astroturf is easily recognized as artificial.

Grassroots group members outside the Senate chambers on their lobby day.

Active members: Members of a group who are actively involved. Active members tend to go to group meetings, serve on subcommittees and as officers, and generally do the ongoing work of the group.

Auxiliary members: People who, while nominally group members or interested in a group's work, typically are less involved with the group than active members. However, auxiliary members can often be relied on for special efforts, such as telephone, letter, or e-mail campaigns, if they are sufficiently motivated by the efforts of group officers and active members. Auxiliary members out-number active members in almost every grassroots organization. Note that some groups formally designate auxiliary members, but we are concerned here with a more informal designation.

Getting Organized and Getting Busy

Just as there is no single best structure for a group, there is no single best way to get one started. The impetus may come from a single, highly motivated citizen, from a couple of neighbors talking over the back fence, or from a community organization or leader. Regardless of how a group starts, to survive and pursue its policy goals effectively, it needs organization.

The first step in organizing a potential group is to define its goals and purpose. What does your group want out of the public policy process? To repeal or enact a particular law? To have a long-term impact on a variety of laws in a policy area? Does your group want to influence the state legislature, a city council, state or local executive agencies, or all of these? Who you target will depend on who controls the policy decisions that your group wants to influence. Being clear and specific in your goals and the targets of your future activity from the outset will focus and energize your group, decrease future intra-group squabbling, and enhance your overall effectiveness in the policy-making process.

Broadening your group's membership base is almost always a good idea. Usually the more members you have, the greater the potential for political impact. Recruitment can be handled several ways. You may make a general call for volunteers or recruit members selectively. Seek out persons and groups with an interest in and concern about your group's issue. Good sources of group members are service groups, civic volunteers, community organizations, churches, neighbors, family, and friends. Talk with people about your group's issue, formally and informally. You will find like-minded

people in the places you normally go.

Citizen groups generally have two types of members: **active members** — those who attend meetings and do the ongoing work of the group — and **auxiliary members** — those who do not take a regular, active role, but who can be relied on for special efforts, such as telephone, letter, or e-mail campaigns. While groups don't usually classify their members this way officially, it is often clear to which category most members belong. While your active members will drive group operations, don't underestimate or downplay the importance of your auxiliary members. They are the foot soldiers needed for your group's activities.

Once a nucleus of volunteers has been formed, a group must decide on the basic structure that is most appropriate to its goals and members. A loosely structured group holds infrequent meetings, develops few, if any, publications and mailings, and communicates with legislators only on a very limited number of issues. The chairperson or president may be chosen by consensus and may do most of the group's work, perhaps with the help of a few other active members. A highly structured group has formally selected officers, holds regular meetings and other activities, formulates clear positions, and communicates these positions regularly to legislators. Most groups' structures fall somewhere between these two extremes.

Group organizers also need to consider other organizational issues when deciding on the appropriate structure to meet their goals:

- **Finances.** Many grassroots groups operate on a shoestring budget, so the lack of funding should not discourage a group from forming. Typical expenses include postage, telephone bills, printing costs, and refreshments for meetings and activities. Members often donate these services. Revenue can be generated through membership dues or through traditional fundraising activities like car washes and bake sales. Note that, depending on a group's potential membership, dues may hurt recruitment, while social fundraising activities may actually encourage people to join. Since the crucial resource of a grassroots group is its membership, not its bank account, the effect of revenue-raising activities on membership levels needs to be considered carefully.

• **Motivation.** Will members' motivation sustain regular, continuing activities, or can these people be counted on only for brief spurts of effort? If the latter is the case, leaders must reserve their members' energy and resources for critical activities only. It is also important for leaders to understand the motivational level of different members. A leader may rely on the few, highly motivated and more active members to plan and organize the group's activities, mobilizing the least active auxiliary members for instances when a lot of people are needed for short-lived activities, such as a rally or a telephone campaign.

• **Sustaining interest.** Given all the competition for people's attention in today's busy and complex world, group leaders must think creatively and continually about stimulating and sustaining members' interest in the group and its cause. Trips to the Statehouse, candidate forums, and meetings that feature informative speakers not only help keep members current and their interest high, they can also serve to develop the personal contacts needed in lobbying.

For groups with electronically inclined members, online discussions and chat rooms may provide a means of sustaining interest and keeping members up-to-date on the issues.

• **Education.** Group members need a working knowledge of the legislative process and how to approach legislators, as well as factual information about the group's issues. This is crucial to the success of the group's

A grassroots group member explains her case to a senator at a Statehouse rally.

legislative agenda, since ill-informed members can often do more harm than good by alienating policy-makers or miscommunicating your group's message. An important part of an effective group's mission is to inform and train its own members on the issues and the policy-making process.

• **Maintenance.** Even in the most loosely organized group, someone must maintain membership lists, initiate recruitment activities, alert members to issues, call meetings, and so forth. This often falls to the leader who is most motivated and best organized. Without someone to take responsibility for the group's records and duties, the group will not stay together, much less be effective in pursuing its policy goals.

• **Media involvement.** Public relations and media coverage are among the most important tools grass-roots organizations have in their efforts to influence policy-making. A well-planned, consistent message presented by a group at newsworthy events, such as press conferences, demonstrations, and workshops, can gen-

erate the sort of publicity that cannot be bought. Send well-informed and well-written press releases and letters to the editor to your local media. Invite reporters to special events, such as candidate forums or speeches by lawmakers (but make sure that your speakers are informed in advance that the press has been invited). Legislators and candidates generally like media coverage, and they may even be more likely to make an appearance if they know reporters will be there.

Timing is crucial when working with the media. For example, if press releases and letters come too frequently, the media may begin to regard your group as a bunch of crackpots and not take you seriously. If you invite legislators or candidates to speak at an event, send out a press release about one or two weeks in advance.

If you want TV news coverage, time the event to make it convenient for them, at least two or three hours before a regular newscast. Call to remind the station news director the morning of your event.

• **Non-partisanship vs. direct political action.** If a group has decided to be non-partisan, its leaders must monitor its activities scrupulously to ensure that it remains non-partisan. This means not involving itself financially with any political party, being balanced in its assessment of candidates on the policy positions they espouse, and generally maintaining a policy focus in its activities rather than focusing on elections. Failure to do this may affect

Web sites are great tools for grassroots organizations. They are an inexpensive way to get your message out, motivate members, and provide up-to-the-minute information about your issues and group activities to your members, the media, and the public.

the group's tax status and whether or not donations to it are tax-deductible. Perhaps more important, being non-partisan instills a certain credibility in a group with the media and the public, allowing it greater freedom to control its own message. This may be lost if a group is perceived as a "tool" of one party. However, if your group decides to undertake partisan activity, you should seek legal advice before-hand (see Chapter 8).

Tips for Grassroots Organizers

Consider the following tips for organizing grassroots groups:

- **Talk to someone who has grassroots experience**. In fact, talk to several people with such experience. There is no reason to re-invent the wheel. Nor is there any reason to make the same mistakes that other groups have already made. But remember that what has worked for another group might not work for your group.

- **Lobbying can be frustrating—get used to it**. Group members must realize from the outset that lobbying is a frustrating business. Being right is no guarantee of winning. Especially frustrating is the fact that battles that seem to be won sometimes are not. For example, a bill your group opposes may be defeated on the floor, only to sneak through as an amendment to another bill. Conversely, a bill your group supports may pass the legislature only to be vetoed by the governor. A clear understanding of the legislative process will reduce the demoralizing effects of setbacks.

Rallies are often held on the first floor of the Statehouse rotunda during legislative sessions.

• **Don't be intimidated**. Some people think that politicians such as legislators and the governor are out of the reach of ordinary people. On the contrary, they are generally quite approachable. Remember, their profession is listening to citizens and making policy decisions based on the balance of what they hear. Most lawmakers are glad to hear from their constituents—and those

who aren't usually won't be in their positions very long.

• **Keep in touch with legislators year-round**. The best grassroots lobbying often occurs when the legislature is not in session. At these times, lawmakers have more time to listen to groups and perhaps have a little more perspective on what is important to the state and its citizens. Between sessions, they have more time to get

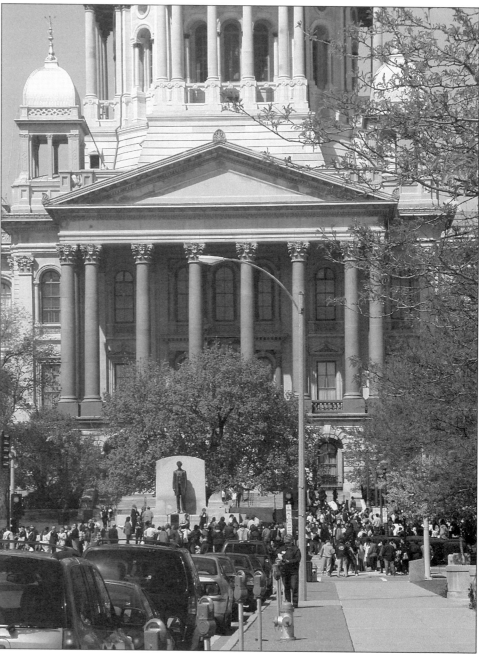

Citizens rally to support their cause at the Statehouse.

to know your group, its leaders, and whom it represents. This is a good time to invite legislators to speak to your group or attend your group's events. When appropriate, send notes of praise and encouragement to legislators, both directly and publicly through the local media.

• **Anticipate that maintaining member and media interest will be a problem**. Some hot topics generate their own interest, but some of the most important public policy issues are not very exciting to most people. The appropriations process is a notable example of this. It is hard to understand and harder still to follow the various bills that affect it, but almost nothing is more important in the policy-making process. Be prepared to sell the importance of your issues and positions continually—to policy-makers, to group members, and to the media. But don't expect everyone to be as interested in your group and your issues as you are.

• **Train members who will have contact with policy-makers and the media.** Be sure all your group members know the basics of how to approach legislators and have solid background information before they begin writing letters or charging the Statehouse. Offensive, aggressive, or ill-informed members can destroy a group's credibility very quickly.

• **Pace membership activities**. To succeed in the policy-making process, a steady effort is needed at every step, right up to the moment the governor acts on a bill or an administrative rulemaking is completed. Group members may be inclined to squander their enthusiasm in the opening stages of the process. Effective group leaders shepherd their members' energy and use it where and when in the long process it is most needed.

• **Don't expect to win every time**. Nobody wins all the time in politics. It is an ongoing, never-ending process that allows some wins and some losses for most groups from time to time. When you lose, learn from it. What could you have done differently? What seemed to work for the opposing side? Above all, do not take defeat personally. There are many forces at work in the policy-making process, and you can't blame yourself, or any other single person, for your defeat. Lose graciously and come back stronger next time.

• **It's not whether you win or lose but how you play the game**. While you and your group have important policy goals, remember that the process is a long and difficult one. On any given bill, rule, or vote, it may often be better to work hard and act cleanly and professionally than to win what might be a short-lived victory. A group that gets a reputation for being untruthful, inflexible, and unable to see the perspective of other players in the process will not be able to maintain an effective and permanent voice in the policy-making process. ❏

chapter 8

Lobbying Laws and Ethics

Lobbying carries a negative connotation for the average American. One prominent lobbyist for an Illinois education organization explains that rather than say he's a lobbyist, his mother tells her friends, "He helps out the teachers." The image of an overstuffed lobbyist in a plaid suit, smoking a big cigar, and currying favor by throwing extravagant parties and doling out envelopes of cash is a strong one in our collective consciousness. But like many popular images, it is an exaggerated stereotype that reflects little of today's reality, even if it may have been more accurate in the past. Today, lobbyists are hardworking professionals who play an important role in the legislative process, a much more open process than in days past. Legislators are under constant media scrutiny. Direct bribery and other such instances of blatant lobbyist misconduct may still happen, but the occurrences are rare, indeed.

Past abuses and this persistent negative public image have led to significant state regulation of lobbyists. Furthermore, lobbyists themselves have developed formal and informal codes of conduct to ensure ethical practices. Lobbyists must work both ethically and legally, not only to

Lobbyists have a poor public image for the average citizen.

avoid prosecution, but also to gain policymakers' respect and confidence, which is crucial to successful lobbying. While not every ethical lobbyist is an effective lobbyist, few unethical lobbyists are effective in the long run.

In this chapter, we provide a brief overview of the legal and ethical issues in lobbying. By no means is this an exhaustive treatment of the subject. If you and your group are considering getting involved in the legislative arena (and particularly in political campaign activities), we strongly recommend that you consult an attorney with expertise in the area.

For up-to-date details on lobbyist registration and other regulations, contact the Illinois Secretary of State's Index Department. Also, keep in mind that the debate over lobbyist and legislator ethics laws and rules is anticipated to continue, resulting in further legal and administrative implications for lobbyists.

Regulations and the Right to Lobby

Some people may be wary of getting involved in lobbying for fear they will violate some law they are unaware of. Such fears are unfounded. Any citizen is free to communicate at any time with any legislative body or any individual legislator on virtually any issue. Lobbying regulations do not in any way abridge the right of citizens to petition their government. In fact, in the interest of good government, such communications are more than a right— they are a duty.

Special laws only regulate people who get involved in the legislative process if *either:*

1. They accept compensation to represent someone else's views before the legislature, such as if they are

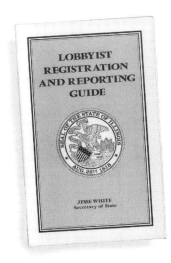

The *Lobbyist Registration and Reporting Guide* provides vital information on how to register and report lobbying expenditures. It is available free of charge from the Secretary of State's Index Department.

employed by a statewide organization. Lobbyists in this category must register and file regular reports with the secretary of state (see the discussion of lobbyist registration on pages 102-10).

or

2. They participate in an election campaign by raising funds for a candidate, publicly endorsing a candidate, or spending funds to pass or defeat a referendum issue. Depending on the extent of these activities, such people may be required to keep records and file reports (see the discussion of election activities on pages 111-14).

On the other hand, citizens *can* do the following in supporting or opposing legislation without dealing with any government regulations:

• Communicate their own views to state officials and other citizens; and

• Form and join groups that work together to communicate their views to the legislature and the public.

Citizens who band together may find it advantageous to incorporate as a not-for-profit organization. Such organizations may obtain certain benefits, such as being able to accept tax-deductible, charitable contributions. On the other hand, special laws regulate the amount of money that may be spent in direct lobbying by not-for-profit charitable organizations, and considerable record keeping is required. Citizens considering the pros and cons of establishing formal organizations should consult an attorney.

The Lobbyist Registration Act

The Lobbyist Registration Act (25 ILCS 170/) specifies the legal responsibilities of lobbyists and organizations involved in lobbying in Illinois. See the secretary of state's free publication, *Lobbyist Registration and Reporting Guide*, for further details on how to register and report lobbying expenses.

Lobbying – The Legal Definition

According to the Lobbyist Registration Act (25 ILCS 170/2), lobbying is:

> any communication with an official of the executive or legislative branch of State government as defined in section (c) for the ultimate purpose of influencing executive, legislative, or administrative action.

Section (c) defines an "**official**" as the governor; lieutenant governor; secretary of state; attorney general; state treasurer; state comptroller; their chiefs of staff; cabinet members of any elected constitutional officer, including directors, assistant directors, chief legal counsel, and general counsel; and members of the General Assembly.

Any person, firm, partnership, committee, association, corporation, or other organization of persons that "for compensation or otherwise, either individually or as an employee or contractual employee of another person, undertakes to influence executive, legislative or administrative action" is required to register as a lobbyist with the secretary of state "within 10 working days of an agreement to conduct any lobbying activity." Any person, firm, partnership, committee, association, corporation, or other organization of persons that employs another person to lobby state officials must also register with the secretary of state (25 ILCS 170/3). Such a person or group employing a lobbyist is known as an **entity**.

While this definition and registration requirement may seem broad and inclusive, there are many exemptions, and these exemptions are especially pertinent to grassroots lobbying groups. To determine whether you and your group are exempt from the registration requirement, see Section 4 of the Lobbyist Registration Act, consult the secretary of state's office,

Official: As defined in the Lobbyist Registration Act (25 ILCS 170/2c), "officials" are the governor; lieutenant governor; secretary of state; attorney general; state treasurer; state comptroller; their chiefs of staff; cabinet members of any elected constitutional officer, including directors, assistant directors, chief legal counsel, and general counsel; and members of the General Assembly.

Entity: Any person, firm, partnership, committee, association, corporation, or other organization of persons that employs another person to lobby state officials. Entities must be registered in accordance with the Lobbyist Registration Act (25 ILCS 170/3).

Exemptions from lobbyist registration

The Lobbyist Registration Act specifies a variety of exemptions from its lobbyist registration requirement (25 ILCS 170/4). These include:

- Those who lobby without compensation and who do not make reportable expenditures (such as substantial gifts to officials and campaign contributions, as defined in 25 ILCS 170/6).
- Those who work for the media and publish or broadcast editorial comments as part of their journalistic duties.
- Those who provide professional bill drafting and policy analysis services.
- Employees of the state government explaining to officials how a policy will affect their agency.
- Employees of the General Assembly's members, legislative agencies, and legislative commissions.
- Those whose technical skills and knowledge would be helpful to officials when considering policy, who lobby on a limited basis on behalf of a registered lobbyist or group and do not make any reportable expenditures.
- Full-time employees of a religious organization lobbying solely to protect the right of its members to practice their religion.
- Attorneys representing clients in any administrative or judicial proceeding or witnesses providing testimony in such a proceeding.
- Those who are or seek to be a vendor to the state who solicit an official to purchase goods or services where the solicitation is limited to either an oral inquiry or written advertisement and informative literature; the goods and services are subject to competitive bidding requirements; or the goods and services do not cost more than $5,000 and where such persons do not make reportable expenditures.

The Illinois Administrative Code further defines these exemptions (2 Illinois Administrative Code 560.210).

Authorized agent: The person employed by a lobbying entity who is responsible for seeing that each lobbyist is registered, expenditure reports are filed, and the Secretary of State's Index Department is notified of any changes in lobbyists, address, termination of registration, or change of authorized agent.

Client: Any corporation, association, or person that hires a lobbyist or a lobbying entity to lobby on its behalf. Clients must register in accordance with the Lobbyist Registration Act (25 ILCS 170/3).

or get other legal advice. It is especially important to note that the law reiterates the right of citizens under the United States Constitution "to petition" the government and under the Illinois Constitution "to make known their opinions to their representatives and to apply for redress of grievances."

Lobbyist Registration

Those lobbyists and employers of lobbyists who are not exempt from the Lobbyist Registration Act's requirements must register each year (or "before any such service is performed which requires the person to register") by filing a written statement with the secretary of state on or before January 31. Persons employed after that date contractually or as new hires must register within 10 days of the lobby-

ing agreement or employment.

The registration form for employers is the Entity Registration Statement. This statement requires the name and address of the employer, identification of the **authorized agent**, a list of all lobbyists employed, a list of all **clients** retained, and a brief description of lobbying intent, all certified by the designated authorized agent. Clients of private contract lobbyists must also register using the Entity Registration Statement. There is an annual registration fee for each registration of an employer, lobbyist, or client. Lobbyists register using the Exclusive Lobbyist Information Statement. This statement requires the lobbyist's name and address, the name and address of the employing entity, a brief description of the lobbyist's intended activities, and a current photo.

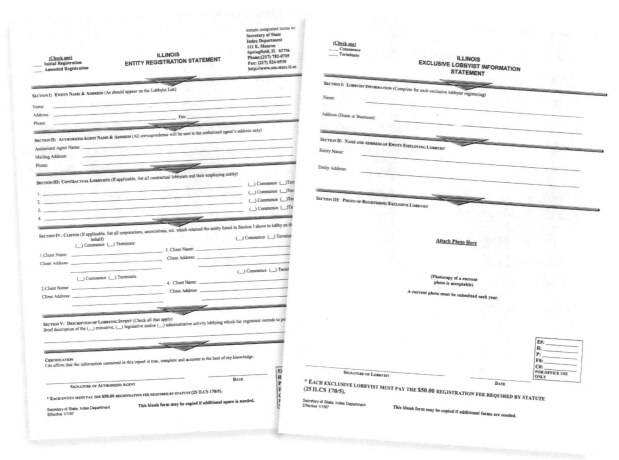

Entity Registration Statement and Exclusive Lobbyist Information Statement forms must be filed with the Secretary of State's Index Department by January 31 each year.

Reporting Requirements

A lobbyist may incur expenses directly related to a specific official, such as taking the official to dinner, offering a gift, or providing an **honorarium** to speak at an event. These expenses may be incurred in the course of advocating a particular policy position or just to generate **goodwill** with the official. Registered entities and lobbyists are required to file expenditure reports of such expenses with the Secretary of State's Index Department twice a year (25 ILCS 170/6). Expenditures made between January 1 and June 30 (or the final day of the spring legislative session, whichever is later) must be reported by July 31. A full report is due January 31 for all expenditures made in the previous calendar year, including those reported on July 31. These reports must be filed even if there are no expenditures made during a reporting period.

Not every expense made in a lobbying effort is reportable. **Non-reportable expenditures** include:

- Reasonable expenses of a registrant for personal sustenance, lodging, travel, office expenses, and clerical

Honorarium: A payment to a person for an appearance or speech, excluding any actual and necessary travel expenses incurred by the person (and one relative). The Illinois Governmental Ethics Act (5 ILCS 420/2-110) prohibits members of the General Assembly from accepting honoraria.

Goodwill: An expenditure made on behalf of an official that has no direct relation to a specific executive, legislative, or administrative action but is made to help establish a positive rapport with that official.

Non-reportable expenditures: Lobbying expenses that do not have to be reported in the semi-annual expenditure reports to the Secretary of State's Index Department. These include membership dues; campaign contributions; a lobbyist's personal expenses; office clerical or support staff expenses; and salaries, fees, and other compensation paid to a registrant for lobbying.

Registration tips

1. You must register by January 31 of each year during which lobbying activity is anticipated.
2. All clients and contractual lobbyists listed on an entity's registration must be registered with the Secretary of State's Index Department.
3. There is a registration fee for each entity and individual who lobbies exclusively for that entity.
4. Submit only one check to the Index Department for the total amount owed by your entity.
5. All registrations made during the calendar year expire on December 31 regardless of the date they are filed.
6. Registrations may be terminated before December 31 if the authorized agent notifies the Index Department in writing and a final expenditure report is submitted with the termination.
7. Client or lobbyist additions must be filed with the Index Department within 10 working days.
8. Changes to a registration, such as a change of mailing address or authorized agent, must be filed with the Index Department within 30 days.

SOURCE: Jesse White, Illinois Secretary of State, *Lobbyist Registration and Reporting Guide*, May 1999, p. 8

A state senator meets with a group at the Statehouse.

Exclusive lobbyist: An employee of a registered entity who engages in direct lobbying only for that entity regardless of the number of hours per week he or she devotes to lobbying.

Contractual lobbyist: A person or firm hired by one or more entities to lobby on its behalf. Contractual lobbyists must register in accordance with the Lobbyist Registration Act (25 ILCS 170/3).

Itemized expenditure: Any individual expenditure for or on behalf of an official exceeding $100 that is listed separately on the Illinois Expenditure Report Itemized Schedule.

Non-itemized expenditure: Any individual expenditure for or on behalf of an official of less than $100 that is combined with other non-itemized expenditures on the Illinois Expenditure Summary Report.

Large gathering: An event held by a registered entity to which 25 or more officials are invited. Expenses for such events are reported on the Illinois Expenditure Report Large Gatherings or Giveaways Schedule.

Giveaway: A substantially similar gift given to 25 or more officials at one time. Expenses for such giveaways are reported on the Illinois Expenditure Report Large Gatherings or Giveaways Schedule.

and support staff;
• Salaries, fees, and other compensation paid to the registrant for the purpose of lobbying;
• Contributions required to be reported under Article 9 of the Election Code;
• Reasonable expenses of attending and participating in commission or committee meetings or hearings for registrants who are members of a legislative or state study commission or committee; and
• Gifts and honoraria returned to the registrant within 30 days of the date of receipt.

Who reports a given expenditure on his or her report? That depends on who actually makes the expenditure. Specifically:

• If an expenditure is made by a

> **Remember**: Each registered lobbyist and entity must submit an expenditure report twice a year, even if no reportable expenditures were incurred during a reporting period.

registered entity or by that entity's **exclusive lobbyist**, then the registereed entity reports the expenditure.
• If an expenditure is made by a **contractual lobbyist** and the lobbyist was not reimbursed by a client, then the contractual lobbyist reports the expenditure.
• If an expenditure is made by a contractual lobbyist and the lobbyist was reimbursed by a client, then the client reports the expenditure.

Entities and lobbyists are required to file expenditure reports using the Expenditure Summary Report form to summarize all lobbying expenses made in a reporting period. Depending on the types of expenses, additional schedules and statements may also need to be completed. Expenditures are listed as **itemized expenditures** and **non-itemized expenditures**

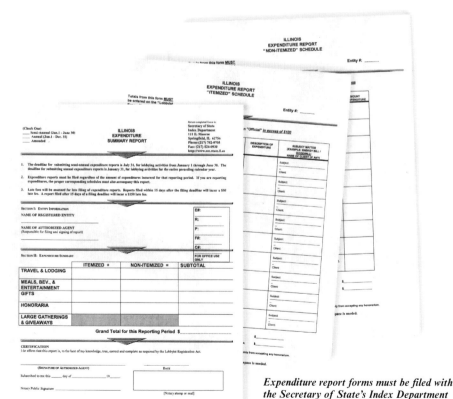

Expenditure report forms must be filed with the Secretary of State's Index Department twice a year.

and divided into five categories: travel and lodging; meals, beverages, and entertainment; gifts; honoraria; and **large gatherings** and **giveaways**. Single expenditures of more than $100 made on behalf of an official or a member of that official's immediate family must be itemized. Non-itemized expenditures are those of $100 or less. These need not be reported individually, but must be categorized and reported in an aggregate total for each official receiving an expenditure.

While itemized and non-itemized expenditures are reported separately for each official who receives them, large gatherings and giveaways only need to be reported by event, as long as 25 or more officials were invited to attend the gathering or received the giveaway. The Large Gatherings or Giveaways Schedule must be filed to indicate whether the expendi-

> Members of the General Assembly are prohibited from accepting honoraria (5 ILCS 420/2-110).

ture was for an event or a giveaway, the amount of the expenditure, the date, the number of people attending the event, and the number of officials attending the event or receiving the giveaway. Gatherings hosted by more than one registered lobbying entity may be prorated to reflect each entity's portion.

Entities with a grassroots component must also file a Grass Roots Lobbying Statement on behalf of each member organization or individual that incurs a reportable expenditure from a **grassroots lobbying communication** or a **grassroots lobbying event**. The entity is responsible for informing participants in writing that any reportable expenditures must be disclosed to its authorized agent within 30 days of the event. The Grass Roots Lobbying Statement reports the name of the entity sponsoring the grassroots

Grassroots lobbying communication: Any correspondence by a registered entity that encourages further correspondence to an official in support of or opposition to an issue, as well as the ensuing correspondence by the individuals. The entity must make participants in this process aware of the Illinois Grass Roots Lobbying Statement for any reportable expenses they incur.

Grassroots lobbying event: Any organized activity sponsored by a registered entity intended to influence the action of officials by inviting participants to a location where officials are accessible. The entity must make participants in such an event aware of the Illinois Grass Roots Lobbying Statement for any reportable expenses they incur.

This form must be filed to supplement the lobbying expenditure reports to document large gathering or giveaway expenses.

This form must be completed by grassroots group members who incur reportable expenses and then is filed with the entity's lobbying expenditure report.

lobbying event or communication; the date; the name, address, and telephone number of the person who made the reportable expenditure; a list of the officials or the officials' family members on whose behalf the expenditure was made; and the amount spent. The participant who made the reportable expenditure completes the statement, signs it, and returns it to the authorized agent for filing as an addendum to the entity's report. If a participant incurring a reportable expenditure fails to return the statement to the registered entity (or if the registered entity refuses to claim sponsorship of the event), the participant is personally subject to the lobbyist registration and reporting requirements (2 Illinois Administrative Code 560.325 and 326).

All lobbyist reporting and expenditure forms are available from the Secretary of State's Index Department and may be downloaded at http://www.sos.state.il.us/departments/index/lobbyist_page.html

The Illinois Secretary of State's Index Department handles lobbyist registration and reporting. Index Department offices are located across the street from the Statehouse at 111 E. Monroe St. in Springfield.

Notice to Officials

A lobbyist or entity must send two notices to each official on whose behalf expenditures were made for each reporting period (25 ILCS 170/6.0 and 6.5; 2 Illinois Administrative Code 560.372). The first notice must be sent by first class mail or hand delivery at least 25 days before the filing deadline for the report—January 6 for the annual report and July 6 for the mid-year report. This notice must include the total amount of each expenditure, the date incurred, and the subject matter of the lobbying activity, if any. This report may be simply a copy of the relevant Illinois Expenditure Report Itemized Schedule. The second notice must be provided within 30 days after the filing deadline—March 2 for the annual report and August 30 for the mid-year report. These notices provide the official with the opportunity to challenge the lobbying expenditure reports, if the official desires to do so.

Duties of a Registered Lobbyist or Authorized Agent

A registered lobbyist or an entity's authorized agent is responsible for maintaining up-to-date registration information and filing accurate expenditure reports. This includes forwarding any changes in the initial registration and changes or corrections in the expenditure reports, schedules, and statements to the Secretary of State's Index Department. Changes or corrections in the expenditure reports, schedules, and statements must be made within 30 days of such changes on the appropriate form(s) and marked "amended." In addition, all receipts and records used in preparing the expenditure reports, schedules, and statements must be kept for two years from the filing date of the reports. According to the Illinois Administrative Code (25 ILCS 170/6; 2 Illinois Administrative Code 560.375 and 395), the records that must be kept include, but are not limited to:

- The total of all expenditures made for or on behalf of officials;
- Proof of payment for each expenditure in excess of $100;
- The allocation formula used in prorating an expenditure that was made for more than one official, but fewer than 25 officials; and
- A list of the officials invited to a large gathering.

The lobbyist or authorized agent is also required to notify the Secretary of State's Index Department of the termination of lobbying by the entity or any of its lobbyists within 30 days of the termination (25 ILCS 170/6; 2 Illinois Administrative Code 560.385). When the entity terminates lobbying, the written notice must also include a report of expenditures from the last reporting period until the date of termination. If the termination is of a lobbyist, that lobbyist is responsible for providing a report of the expenditures to the entity within 30 days of termination, and the entity is responsible for including those expenditures in the entity's next report.

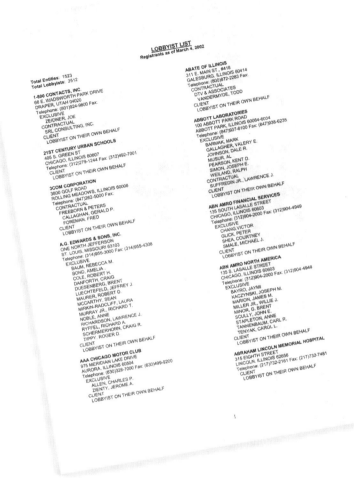

The updated list of registered lobbyists and entities can be downloaded from the Secretary of State's Index Department's Web site at: http://www.sos.state.il.us/departments/index/lobbyist_page.html.

Public Access to Registration and Reporting Information

The secretary of state is required to keep copies of lobbyist registration and reporting information for three years and make them available to the general public. Requests for this information can be made in person or in writing, and any copies must be paid for in advance. Paper copies of the Lobbyist List and Lobbyist Cross Reference List are available free of charge

Secretary of State's Index Department contact information

Secretary of State
Index Department
Lobbyist Division
111 East Monroe Street
Springfield, IL 62756
Telephone: (217) 782-0643
Web site: http://www.sos.state.il.us/departments/index/lobbyist_page.html
Hours: Monday–Friday, 8am-4:30pm (except legal state holidays)

from the Secretary of State's Index Department or on computer disk for a small fee. Most conveniently, the Lobbyist List and the Lobbyist Cross Reference List may be downloaded from the Index Department's Web site at http://www.sos.state.il.us/departments/index/lobbyist_page.html.

Contingency Fees

In addition to registration and reporting requirements, the Illinois Lobbyist Registration Act prohibits clients and entities from compensating lobbyists based on their policy-making accomplishments. For example, a client may not hire a lobbyist for a specific fee and then agree to pay a bonus based on the successful passage of a bill (25 ILCS 170/8). Such **contingency fees**, which are common in the legal profession, are outlawed for lobbyists not only in Illinois, but also in most other states.

Penalties

Failure to register or file expenditure reports on time can result in late filing fees, which increase substantially after more than 15 days past a deadline (2 Illinois Administrative Code 560.390). Entities that register within 30 days after an expenditure report deadline have an additional 30 days to file without a late fee. The director of the Secretary of State's Index Department may also grant a

30-day extension for good cause. Within 10 days of failing to register or report expenditures, the Index Department will send a Failure to File notice. If the lobbyist or authorized agent does not respond to this notice, the Office of the Secretary of State will notify the Office of the Attorney General (25 ILCS 170/10; 2 Illinois Administrative Code 560.390).

Any person who violates any of the provisions of the Lobbyist Registration Act, including the failure to register and report expenditures, is guilty of a business offense punishable by a fine of not more than $10,000. In addition, those convicted of a violation of the Act are prohibited from lobbying for three years from the date of the conviction (25 ILCS 170/10; 2 Illinois Administrative Code 560.390).

Lobbying by Charitable Organizations

Some not-for-profit organizations have special status under **Section 501(c)(3)** of the U.S. Internal Revenue Service Code that allows those who make contributions to these groups to deduct those contributions from their taxable income. This is an important advantage because it gives potential donors an incentive to contribute. However, according to U.S. Treasury Regulations, "substantial" lobbying by a tax-exempt organization will result in the loss of 501(c)(3) status. How is "substantial" defined? The courts have tried to use a balancing test here, comparing the amount of lobbying a group does with its other activities. The only case that gives a specific standard is *Seasongood v. Commissioner*, 227 F.2d 907 (6th Cir. 1955), in which the court held that "less than five percent of time and effort" was not substantial within the meaning of 501(c)(3).

For further information on the Lobbyist Registration Act, refer to 25 Illinois Compiled Statutes 170/, 2 Illinois Administrative Code 560, and the *Lobbyist Registration and Reporting Guide*. Copies of the statute and administrative rules are available from the Secretary of State's Index Department and may be downloaded from its Web site (http://www.sos.state.il.us/departments/index/lobbyist_page.html). The Index Department anticipates that the Web site will eventually include the *Lobbyist Registration and Reporting Guide*.

The decision was not based merely on a comparison of funds expended, but also on a comparison of time and effort involved in lobbying and nonlobbying activities.

Although *Seasongood* is not controlling outside the Sixth U.S. Circuit, and despite the vagueness of other case law and regulations, charitable organizations can probably operate a legislative program without challenge if the time and resources spent on lobbying do not exceed five percent of that spent on all other projects. Furthermore, there are no cases that suggest that the IRS regulations are intended to limit appearances by group members or officers at public hearings to explain the effects of legislation or to offer information at any time if requested by a legislator.

Not-for-profit organizations that concentrate heavily on legislative reform or "good government" policy lobbying can adopt an approach suggested by Section 501(c)(4) of the IRS Code. That section exempts "civil leagues or organizations not organized for profit but operated exclusively for the promotion of social welfare" from paying federal taxes and imposes no limitations on their political activities (Treasury Regulations 1.501(c)(4)—1). However, there remains this important distinction between 501(c)(3) and 501(c)(4) organizations— a person can take a tax deduction for a donation to the former but not the latter. A tax-exempt organization can retain its 501(c)(3) status and still engage in a great deal

of legislative activity if a splinter group is organized under 501(c)(4) and if that group is organized and operates completely apart from the 501(c)(3) program. In such a case, money donated to the 501(c)(3) component of the group could be tax-deductible but not donations to the 501(c)(4) component. It is imperative to get specific legal and financial advice before taking any action in this regard.

Election Activity

Any group thinking about getting involved in elections should obtain legal advice before initiating any activities, including contributing money to campaigns, making public endorsements, or even encouraging group members to vote or volunteer for a candidate's campaign.

There are distinct pros and cons to election activity. On the pro side, your group may gain easier access to an elected official you help get elected, or you may help elect a like-minded official who will

Section 501(c)(4) organizations: A class of charitable organizations, contributions to which are *not* tax deductible under the U.S. Internal Revenue Service Code section 501(c)(4). Eligible organizations are "civil leagues or organizations not organized for profit but operated exclusively for the promotion of social welfare." These organizations are exempt from paying federal taxes, and there is no limitation on their political activities.

State legislators are often most comfortable talking to constituents in their districts.

be naturally sympathetic to your cause. On the con side, you may make an enemy in government if your candidate does not win the election, thus reducing your access. More importantly, there are a plethora of legal and ethical issues that campaign activities raise for lobbyists. While a complete survey of these issues is beyond the scope of this book, we raise a few of them to give you a feel for the concerns involved. For further information and ideas on campaign activity, see DeKeiffer (1997) and other books in the "Further Reading on Lobbying and Illinois Government" section after Chapter 9.

Many grassroots groups avoid election activity of any kind. Some do so because they don't want the official responsibilities imposed by the law, some because of the bipartisan or non-partisan nature of their members, and some because they feel that political action conflicts with their mission. However, campaign contributions and assistance can help develop access to policy-makers for groups that might otherwise be unable to attract attention.

Under Article 9 of the Illinois Election Code (10 ILCS 5/9-1), a person, trust, partnership, committee, association, corporation, or other organization or group of persons becomes a **political committee** when:

- It accepts contributions or makes expenditures exceeding a total of $3,000 in any 12-month period on behalf of, or in opposition to, a candidate or candidates for public office; or

- It accepts contributions or makes expenditures exceeding a total of $3,000 in any 12-month period to support or oppose any question of public policy to be submitted to the voters at a referendum; or

- It accepts contributions or makes expenditures exceeding a total of $3,000 in any 12-month period and has as its primary purpose the furtherance of governmental, political, or social values; is organized on a not-for-profit basis; and publicly endorses or publicly opposes a candidate or candidates for public office.

Under the election code, contributions are defined as cash, loans, and in-kind contributions.

A group that qualifies as a political committee under one of these criteria must file a Statement of Organization (D-1 form) with the State Board of Elections and its county clerk, maintain and retain accurate records of contributions and disbursements, file a regular Report of Campaign Contribution and Expenditure (D-2 form), and meet other legal obligations.

Similarly, a not-for-profit organization that meets *all* of the following criteria

State Board of Elections publications

The Illinois State Board of Elections Web site contains, among other things, two important publications for groups thinking about getting involved in campaign activity:

- *A Guide to Campaign Disclosure* describes how to report group campaign activities.
- *Disclosure of Campaign Contributions and Expenditures and Rules and Regulations* describes the specific statutes and rules that pertain to group campaign activity.

These publications can be downloaded free of charge at:

http://www.elections.state.il.us/CDS/pages/References.htm.

must register with the State Board of Elections and disclose certain information similar to the obligations required of political committees. These requirements apply if the not-for-profit group:

- Is not a tax-exempt corporation under the IRS code section 501(c)(3); and
- Is not a labor union; and
- Is registered under the Lobbyist Registration Act or for which lobbying is undertaken by persons registered under that Act; and
- Has not established a political committee; and
- Accepts or spends a total of more than $5,000 during any 12-month period on behalf of, or in opposition to, public officials or candidates for public office or a question of

public policy and for the purpose of influencing legislative, executive, or administrative action as defined in the Lobbyist Registration Act.

Grassroots groups can be active politically without coming under Article 9 of the Election Code if they do not receive or spend more than $3,000 in one year. For example, a group that operates on a budget of less than $3,000 a year may endorse candidates and contribute to political campaign funds without organizing as a political committee. Since many grassroots groups rely on volunteer effort and donated in-kind services and material, this $3,000 minimum means that many grassroots groups may act politically without the reporting and registration requirements of political committees. When the main resource is its members' time and

When a group engages in election activity at a certain level (generally, $3,000 worth of activity per year), it must register as a political committee (using the D-1 form) and file regular financial reports (using the D-2 form) with the State Board of Elections.

effort, this can be a crucial exemption.

It is important to reiterate that any individual or group planning to raise political campaign funds or endorse political candidates should obtain legal advice beforehand to determine the effect of the Election Code on their efforts.

Lobbying Ethics

Beyond the legal requirements of lobbyist registration and reporting are the more amorphous and subjective consider-ations of lobbying ethics. These are the definitions of right and wrong lobbying behavior that are not codified, but rather exist in the values and morals of each lobbyist and public official. We do not presume to tell you what values you ought to uphold as a lobbyist. But we discuss some ethical guidelines that others have developed and consider the implications these guidelines have for effective lobbying. We believe that, even though ethical lobbying is not always effective, in the long run, unethical lobbying is always ineffective.

The American League of Lobbyists' "Code of Ethics"

Article I- Honesty and Integrity

A lobbyist should conduct lobbying activities with honesty and integrity.

Article II- Compliance with Applicable Laws, Rules, and Regulations

A lobbyist should seek to comply fully with all laws, regulations, and rules applicable to the lobbyist.

Article III- Professionalism

A lobbyist should conduct lobbying activities in a fair and professional manner.

Article IV- Conflicts of Interest

A lobbyist should not continue or undertake representations that may create conflicts of interest without the informed consent of the client or potential client involved.

Article V- Due Diligence and Best Efforts

A lobbyist should vigorously and diligently advance and advocate the client's or employer's interests.

Article VI- Compensation and Engagement Terms

An independent lobbyist who is retained by a client should have a written agreement with the client regarding the terms and conditions for the lobbyist's services, including the amount of and basis for compensation.

Article VII- Confidentiality

A lobbyist should maintain appropriate confidentiality of client or employer information.

Article VIII- Public Education

A lobbyist should seek to ensure better public understanding and appreciation of the nature, legitimacy, and necessity of lobbying in our democratic governmental process. This includes the First Amendment right to "petition the government for redress of grievances."

Article IX- Duty to Governmental Institutions

In addition to fulfilling duties and responsibilities to the client or employer, a lobbyist should exhibit proper respect for the governmental institutions before which the lobbyist represents and advocates clients' interests.

For a more detailed exposition of this Code of Ethics, see the American League of Lobbyists Web site at http://www.alldc.org/ethicscode.htm.

Furthermore, those who engage in ethical lobbying help to enhance the image of all those who lobby, which promotes the interests of government, public policy, and the citizens of Illinois.

Codes of Ethics

The American League of Lobbyists and the American Society of Association Executives are national organizations that promote lobbying as a profession. Both groups have developed a code of conduct or ethics for their members. While the specifics differ, the basic thrust of these standards focuses on several key points. An ethical lobbyist:

- Provides complete and accurate information to policy-makers, to the best of his or her knowledge;
- Complies with all lobbying laws and regulations relevant to the official being lobbied;
- Acts in a professional and respectful manner in all lobbying activities;
- Understands and respects the officials and institutions being lobbied;
- Avoids representing clients whose interests conflict;
- Maintains the confidentiality of client information; and
- Gives his or her best efforts to represent the group or client.

An ethical lobbyist works for the long-term best interests of the group or client, and in doing so works in the long-term best interests of the policy-makers being lobbied and the citizens of Illinois. You can see this best by imagining the impact of a lobbyist violating one of these ethical standards. A lobbyist who misrepresents information may not be trusted the next time he or she makes a case. The lobbyist who disrespects an official may lose access to that official and other

officials, and thus may lose influence. A lobbyist who has conflicts of interest among his or her clients may not be able to represent each effectively and may lose credibility with policy-makers. In short, we suggest that you follow these codes of ethical conduct not only to enhance the credibility of the lobbying profession, but also to gain the personal respect and credibility necessary to be an effective lobbyist.

The Ethical and Legal Concerns of Those You Lobby

Beyond these basic ethical standards, we believe that to maintain your own ethical balance, you should think about the ethical considerations of *those you lobby.* Put yourself in the place of these officials. Legally, what can they do and not do? What might embarrass them, even if it is legal? What would make them uncomfortable if it appeared on the front page of their local newspaper? What actions might violate their personal codes of conduct?

Members of the General Assembly and other state officials are covered by at least two laws that may impact their interest in receiving gifts and other expenditures from a lobbyist. You should familiarize yourself with these statutes and follow closely any changes in these and other relevant laws.

First, the Illinois Governmental Ethics Act (5 ILCS 420/) requires state officeholders and candidates to file with the secretary of state annual statements listing their economic interests. This is done to make the public aware of any conflicts of economic interest. Most relevant to lobbyists, officials and candidates must report the source of gifts totaling over $500 in a calendar year and whether any partner or business associate is a compensated lobbyist (Note: This does not include campaign contributions.) This Act also bans legislators from lobbying for compensation, accepting compensation (other than their official salaries and allowances) for performing their official duties, and accepting honoraria.

Another statute affecting the lobbyist-legislator relationship is the State Gift Ban Act (5 ILCS 425/), which took effect in 1999. This Act states that a legislator, his or her spouse, and his or her immediate family cannot solicit or accept any "gifts" from "prohibited sources," both of which are defined in the Act. Essentially, the Act defines "gifts" as anything of tangible or intangible value. But the Act also provides for a long list of exceptions, such as tennis and golf outings and gifts of nominal value, such as tee shirts and plaques. There are also a variety of "prohibited

American Society of Association Executives' "Standards of Conduct"

- The association lobbyist accepts the fact that it is the system of representative government we enjoy that makes possible the practice of lobbying and, while keeping the interest of employer or client in a position of primacy, will temper the advocacy role with proper consideration for the general public interest.

- The association lobbyist will protect confidences, not only those of the employers or client, but also those of elected and appointed officials of government and professional colleagues.

- The association lobbyist will always deal in accurate, current, and factual information, whether it is being reported to the employer or client, government officials, the media, or professional colleagues, and will not engage in misrepresentation of any nature.

- The association lobbyist will acquire enough knowledge of public policy issues to be able to present all points of view fairly.

- The association lobbyist will avoid conflicts of interest, not only conflicts with the interests of the employer or client, but also with those of colleagues pursuing the same or similar objectives, and, where conflict is unavoidable, will communicate the facts fully and freely to those affected.

- The association lobbyist will comply with the laws and regulations governing lobbying, as well as the standards of conduct applying to officials and staff of the Congress, the Executive Branch, and the individual states, and will strive to go one step further and function in a manner that goes beyond these official enactments and promulgations.

- The personal conduct of the association lobbyist should not bring discredit to the profession, government, or individual colleagues.

- The association lobbyist will refrain from any form of discrimination that is legally proscribed or simply generally recognized as such.

- A priority goal of the association lobbyist should be to increase public understanding of the process and this objective should be pursued in every possible way - public appearances, media contacts, articles in company and other publications, and contacts in the normal course of everyday life.

- The association lobbyist should constantly strive to upgrade the necessary skills by every means available, continuing formal education, attendance at meetings, and participation in ad hoc groups with like-minded colleagues.

SOURCE: The American Society of Association Executives Web site at http://www.asaenet.org. To locate the Standards of Conduct, follow these links: Professional Interests Section- Government Relations- Online Resources- Guidelines to Lobbyists.

sources," including registered lobbyists (or anyone who is not, but should be, registered based on the registration requirements discussed earlier in this chapter). However, the Gift Ban Act has been challenged in the courts, so some, if not all, of its provisions may be changed in the near future, either by court order or by the legislature itself.

Beyond legalities, you must be sensitive to the personal ethical codes of legislators and other officials, which vary with each official's conscience, values, and district. For example, while one legislator may be comfortable receiving a gift of Cubs tickets from a lobbyist, another may be embarrassed or even insulted by such a gift. Remember, you must report such gifts in your semi-annual reports, and so they become part of the public record that an opponent or journalist could bring to the attention of the legislator's constituents. Some legislators may want the tickets, but only if they can pay you their face value. This way, you don't have to report the expenditure, since the legislator covered the cost. This may still generate goodwill for you and your group, if, for example, those tickets were particularly difficult to come by. Such subtle benefits as being able to buy tickets to a sold-out game are not quantifiable and, thus, not reportable.

If you would like to make a legal expenditure on an official (for example, take him or her to dinner or give a gift of non-nominal value), the best approach is to ask that official if he or she would be comfortable with you doing so. Better still, you could first ask a member of the official's staff if such a request is appropriate, given the official's values. Never send a gift unannounced (unless it is a nominally valued giveaway to many or all legislators). Consider the embarrassment

it would cause you and the official when the official receives your notice of reporting this expenditure, takes offense, and officially returns the gift and objects to the reported expenditure. Your gesture of intended goodwill has only resulted in the need for a formal apology, which is not the best way to gain access and engender trust in your judgment.

The legal and ethical dimensions of the lobbyist-public official relationship help to define the parameters of acceptable lobbyist behavior. These considerations are not onerous, nor indeed are they far beyond the scope of basic common sense and courtesy. They allow for smooth and more open discussion of the public issues facing Illinois and increase public confidence in the policy-making process. ❑

chapter 9

A Lobbyist's Guide
to Information Resources

Lobbyists are information special-ists. Accessing and managing the flow of information is what they do. To assist you in locating and accessing pertinent information about the legislative process, we have compiled a wide range of resources in this chapter. Given space limitations, we were only able to provide you with a starting point in developing your own toolkit of resources.

Much of the information you need about the legislative process is available online, so we have included the electronic addresses of these resources, when available. You may find that some of these addresses have changed since the publication of this book. In such cases, we have tried to provide enough information to assist you in finding their new locations on the World Wide Web.

References on Illinois Politics and Government

There is a wide range of reference material on Illinois politics and government, much of it free of charge or available in your public library.

Illinois Blue Book

Published by the secretary of state's office in the spring of each even-numbered year, the *Illinois Blue Book* is an essential reference to Illinois state government containing, among other things, photographs and biographies of a host of elected and appointed officials, the Illinois Constitution, a brief chronology of Illinois history, and miscellaneous statistics and information about state and local government. ⮂

Handbook of Illinois Government

Published by the secretary of state's office in odd-numbered years, the *Handbook of Illinois Government* provides the basics of Illinois state government and serves as a great educational resource. It is less comprehensive and much shorter than the *Illinois Blue Book*, and it is published in paperback. ⮂

State of Illinois Web Site

Hosted by the State of Illinois, this Web site provides a wide range of information on Illinois, particularly on government in Illinois. Click on "Government" to access the list of state government Web sites, including the "Legislature," "Constitutional Officers," "Judiciary," and "State Agencies."

Illinois Blue Book and *Handbook of Illinois Government* are free from the secretary of state's office at (217) 782-5763, or for a free copy see http://www.cyberdriveillinois.com/publications/stgovpub.html

The State of Illinois Web site homepage at http://www100.state.il.us/

Legislative Research Unit Publications

Legislative Research Unit
222 S. College, Suite 301
Springfield, IL 62704
Telephone: (217) 782-6851
http://www.legis.state.il.us/
commission/lru/lru_home.
html

Roster of State Government Officials

To purchase the *Roster*, contact *Illinois Issues* at (217) 206-6084, or see http://illinoisissues.uis.edu/roster/roster.html

Illinois Statistical Abstract

To purchase the *Abstract*, contact the Office of Research, College of Commerce and Business Administration, University of Illinois at Urbana-Champaign at (217) 333-2330, or see http://www.cba.uiuc.edu/research/

State of Illinois Telephone Directory

To purchase, contact Central Management Services, Division of Telecommunications, 120 W. Jefferson, Springfield, IL 62702; (217) 524-1029. You can also use the directory free of charge online at: http://www100.state.il.us/government/esearch.cfm. Another source of state officials' telephone numbers is the State of Illinois operator at (217) 782-2000.

Handbook of the Illinois Legislature

The *Handbook* is printed primarily for members of the General Assembly, but a limited number of copies are available to the public. For a free copy, contact one of the following at the Statehouse:
Senate Bill Room:
    Room 406 Statehouse
    Telephone: (217) 782-9778
House Bill Room:
    Room 402A Statehouse
    Telephone: (217) 782-2727

Legislative Research Unit Publications on Illinois Politics and Government

Directory of Illinois State Officials is published in the spring of odd-numbered years by the Legislative Research Unit and serves as the official telephone directory of the General Assembly. It contains the district and Springfield office addresses and telephone numbers of all the members of the General Assembly, committee and commission assignments, and contact information for the legislative agencies, constitutional offices, state agencies, state colleges and universities, judicial agencies, the Illinois Legislative Correspondents' Association, and the Illinois congressional delegation.

Just Numbers is published periodically as an update to the *Directory of Illinois State Officials*. It contains only the names and telephone numbers of the members of the Illinois General Assembly and other state government officials and offices.

County Data Book is published periodically by the Legislative Research Unit. It is a paperback that reports the major demographic, economic, and political statistics of each Illinois county.

Directory of Illinois State Officials and *Just Numbers* are printed primarily for state employees. The *County Data Book* is available to the public in print and online. For more information, contact the Legislative Research Unit. ☞

Federal and State Officers

Published by the Illinois State Board of Elections, this publication lists the elected federal and state officers from Illinois, including their district and office addresses and telephone numbers. For a copy, contact the Illinois State Board of Elections at (217) 782-4141, or at http://www.elections.state.il.us/ElecInfo/Pages/DownOff.htm

Almanac of Illinois Politics

Published biennially by the Abraham Lincoln Presidential Center for Governmental Studies (formerly the Institute for Public Affairs) at the University of Illinois at Springfield, this reference book contains legislator information, political and economic profiles of legislative districts, floor votes, top campaign contributors, and statewide election history. Beginning in 2000, the *Almanac* also includes information on constitutional officers, state Supreme Court justices, and members of Illinois' congressional delegation. To purchase the *Almanac*, call (217) 206-6502, or see http://ipapublications.uis.edu/

Roster of State Government Officials

Published annually in March by *Illinois Issues* magazine at the University of Illinois at Springfield, the *Roster* contains photographs, contact information, and committee assignments for members of the General Assembly, along with contact information for other government officials and staff. ☞

Illinois Statistical Abstract

Published annually by the Bureau of Economic and Business Research, College of Commerce and Business Administration, University of Illinois at Urbana-Champaign, this publication includes current Illinois statistics for population, housing, health, education, employment, economics, business, agriculture, finance, transportation, energy, crime and law enforcement, and parks and recreation. It is available in print and on CD-ROM. ☞

Publications of the State of Illinois

Updated annually, this list includes all of the publications and self-help guides published by the State of Illinois. The Illinois State Library is directed to make these state publications available on the Internet. At press time, the State Library is developing a searchable database for Illinois Government Information (IGI) available in conjunction with *Find-It! Illinois*. Call the Illinois State Library at (217) 782-5870, or see the Illinois Government Information (IGI) database at http://www.findit illinois.org/

Secretary of State Publications and Videos

Last published in 2001, this list contains approximately 175 titles on a wide range of topics including how to access state archives and records, business services offered by the state, literacy information, senior and community services, and vehicle services. Call (217) 782-5763, or see http://www.cyberdrive illinois.com/publications/publications.html

State of Illinois Telephone Directory

Published annually by the Department of Central Management Services, this directory contains two sections, one listing all state government senior staff by department and the other listing state employees by name in alphabetical order. ☞

References on the Illinois General Assembly

In addition to the *Illinois Blue Book, Handbook of Illinois Government, Directory of Illinois State Officials, Just Numbers, Almanac of Illinois Politics, Roster of State Government Officials,* and *State of Illinois Telephone Directory*, there are several resources specific to the Illinois General Assembly.

Handbook of the Illinois Legislature

The *Handbook* is published jointly by the Secretary of the Senate and the Clerk of the House at the beginning of each new General Assembly. This pocket-sized book contains information on the General Assembly's membership, leadership, committees, rules, and staff, as well as information on other Illinois government officials, agencies, and the media. ☞

Illinois General Assembly Web Site

The General Assembly Web site is produced by the Legislative Information System (LIS), a legislative support agency. It provides a host of information, including the status and text of legislation, public acts, Illinois Compiled Statutes, Illinois Constitution, and legislative reports, plus information on members, committees, schedules, rules, journals, roll calls, and transcripts for both the Senate and House. It also offers an audio/video link to the House when it is in session. The Web site carries a disclaimer that it is an information service only and should not be relied on as an official record of action. To obtain the most accurate information, contact the Secretary of the Senate or the Clerk of the House for the printed version of the official publication. ➩

Party Caucus Web Sites

Created by the party leaders in each chamber, these Web sites provide membership and partisan information not available on the General Assembly Web site.

Legislative Synopsis and Digest

Published by the Legislative Reference Bureau every Tuesday afternoon during session, the *Digest* provides a compilation of legislation under consideration by the General Assembly, updated with all activity through the previous Friday. The *Digest* includes an index, cross-references, and bill information. To subscribe, contact the Legislative Reference Bureau, Room 112 Statehouse, Springfield, IL 62706; telephone: (217) 782-6625.

Legislative Research Unit Publications

Preface to Lawmaking is published biennially for new members of the General Assembly. It provides a detailed description of the legislative process; discusses the legislative players, the state budget, and the appropriations process; and gives legislators information on their employment, taxes, ethical concerns, and campaign finance.

Constituent Services Guide was published in 2000 and is designed for use by legislators and their staff in answering constituent questions related to Illinois laws and programs.

Illinois Tax Handbook for Legislators is published annually and is designed for use by legislators. The *Handbook* provides detailed information on federal, state, and local taxes and provides a comparison with other selected states.

1970 Illinois Constitution Annotated for Legislators is published periodically and designed for use by legislators. It provides commentary on, and a detailed index of, the current Illinois Constitution, including key court decisions, laws, and attorney general's opinions.

Visitor's Guide to the Illinois General Assembly is published annually and provides an introduction to the legislative process and the General Assembly. The *Guide* is usually available at the Visitor's Center on the third floor of the Statehouse rotunda.

The General Assembly Web site homepage at http://www.legis.state.il.us/

Party Caucus Web sites:
Senate Republicans: http://www.senategop.state.il.us./
Senate Democrats: http://www.senatedem.state.il.us/
House Democrats: http://www.housedem.state.il.us/index2.htm
House Republicans: http://housegop.state.il.us/index.php3

Illinois Legislative Directory

Published by the Illinois Society of Association Executives (ISAE) at the beginning of each new General Assembly, the *Directory* contains photographs and contact information for the members of the General Assembly, committee assignments, seating arrangements, and more. It is published on behalf of the ISAE's member organizations. ➩

Illinois Legislative Roster

Published biennially by the Association of Illinois Electric Cooperatives, the *Roster* contains photos and contact information for members of the General Assembly and other state government officials. For a copy, call (217) 529-5561

Lobbying and Legislative Process Seminars

Offered annually by the Institute for Legislative Studies at the University of Illinois at Springfield, these day-long workshops provide information on the basics of politics and lawmaking in Illinois. ➩

Master Source Videos

Master Source sells several videocassette and instructional guides that are designed to teach students at the elementary and secondary level about the Illinois legislative process. Call (952) 835-1388, or see http://www.mastersource.cc/

Illinois Legislative Directory
The *Directory* is generally available free from ISAE's member organizations. Orders to purchase the *Directory* are taken at the beginning of each General Assembly. For more information, contact the ISAE at (217) 793-5420, or see http://www.isae.com/legisdir.htm

Lobbying and Legislative Process Seminars
For information about upcoming seminars, contact the Intitute for Legislative Studies at (217) 206-6574, or see http://ils.uis.edu/ and see "Events."

Secretary of the Senate
Room 403 Statehouse
Telephone: (217) 782-5715

Clerk of the House
Room 402 Statehouse
Telephone: (217) 782-8223

Senate Bill Room
Room 406 Statehouse
Telephone: (217) 782-9778

House Bill Room
Room 402A Statehouse
Telephone: (217) 782-2727

Senate Enrolling and Engrossing Office
Room 405 Statehouse
Telephone: (217) 782-6970

House Enrolling and Engrossing Office
Room 420 Statehouse
Telephone: (217) 782-7192

Senate Journal Room
Room 407 Statehouse
Telephone: (217) 782-2461

House Journal Room
Room 424 Statehouse
Telephone: (217) 782-6010

Redistricting Web Site

Created by the Illinois Speaker of the House, this Web site provides information about the 2001 Illinois legislative redistricting process. It provides links to comparative maps and related data before and after the most recent legislative redistricting. The individual legislative party Web sites have additional sources of redistricting information. The 2002-2010 state legislative and congressional maps are also available on the Illinois General Assembly Web site. Redistricting Web site: http://www.ilredistricting.org/main.htm State legislative and congressional district maps: http://www.legis.state.il.us/maps/maps.html

•

Resources about the Legislative Process

These are resources for public and official documents about the Illinois legislative process.

•

Secretary of the Senate and Clerk of the House

As the chief clerical officers of their respective chambers, the Secretary of the Senate and the Clerk of the House are the official sources of legislative information from the General Assembly. They are responsible for having legislation printed, delivering passed legislation to the other chamber or to the governor, keeping minutes of floor debates, and publishing calendars and journals, among many other things. Much of the information you may need can come directly from their offices or from offices under their supervision, including the Bill Rooms, Journal Rooms, Enrolling and Engrossing, Transcription, and the Mail Rooms.

When you visit or call for assistance, let the answering secretary refer you to the appropriate information source. When making a written request, address your letter to the Secretary of the Senate or the Clerk of the House. ℂ

•

Bill Rooms

The Senate and House each have a Bill Room. The information available in the Bill Room varies between the chambers. Staff members at both Bill Rooms will take requests for documents over the telephone, but they prefer a written list. Requests are usually filled while you wait, but they may take longer on session days. Materials are free, with the exception of unusually large orders, and orders are available for pick-up or will be mailed for a fee. The Bill Rooms will not fax materials.

During the legislative session, the Bill Rooms are extremely busy. However, you can usually expect information about a chamber's floor activities to be available 24 to 48 hours after a daily session. When you contact a Bill Room, know exactly what bills or amendments you need, and ask for them by number.

Documents available in the Senate Bill Room

include: Senate bills, amendments adopted by the Senate, House bills currently in the Senate (engrossed), constitutional amendments, rules, calendars, journals, *Status of Legislation (LIS)* reports, the Constitution of the State of Illinois, and (if available) the *Handbook of the Illinois Legislature*. The *Legislative Synopsis and Digest* is also available for use in the Senate Bill Room.

Documents available in the House Bill Room include: House bills, amendments filed in the House, Senate bills currently in the House (engrossed), conference committee reports adopted by the House, House and Senate bills that have passed both chambers (enrolled), resolutions adopted by the House (enrolled and engrossed versions), rules, committee assignments, calendars, journals, *Status ofLegislation (LIS)* reports, the Constitution of the State of Illinois, and (if available) the *Handbook of the Illinois Legislature*. The *Legislative Synopsis and Digest* is also available for use in the House Bill Room. ℂ

•

Enrolling and Engrossing Offices

Each chamber has an Enrolling and Engrossing Office where you can obtain copies of that chamber's bills in the form they were sent to the other chamber (engrossing) or the governor (enrolling). In making your requests, ask for the bills by number and for only a few bills at a time. Be sure that any bills you request have actually passed the relevant chamber(s) before making your request. The Clerk of the House prefers that requests for enrolled and engrossed bills be made to the House Bill Room. ℂ

•

Journal Rooms

Each chamber has a Journal Room supervised by its chief clerical officer. The Journal Room is a repository of items documenting the daily activities of the chamber. Documents available include: rules, calendars, committee assignments, filed conference committee reports (House only), adopted amendments, adopted conference committee reports, roll call votes, and (if available) the *Handbook of the Illinois Legislature*. The Clerk of the House prefers that documents also available in the House Bill Room be obtained in the House Bill Room. ℂ

•

Transcription

Each chief clerical officer is responsible for overseeing the word-for-word transcription of the floor actions for their respective chamber. You may request a transcript by citing the bill number and the day(s) it was debated for the current calendar year by contacting the respective transcription office.

For audiotapes of House committee hearings, contact the Chief Committe Clerk.

For transcripts of floor debate from a previous year, contact the Secretary of State's Index Department. Be sure to confirm any copying charges before completing your request.

Transcriptions of legislative debate from the current calendar year:

Senate Transcription
Room 405 Statehouse
Telephone: (217) 782-6653

House Transcription
Room 418 Statehouse
Telephone: (217) 782-1038

Transcriptions of legislative debate from a previous calendar year:

Secretary of State's Index Department
111 East Monroe
Springfield, IL 62756
Telephone: (217) 782-7017

•

Mail Rooms

Each legislative chamber has a mail room through which all mail for legislators is distributed. To save on postage, materials distributed to every member of the chamber may be delivered in bulk to the respective mail room. However, such mass mail drops must be approved by the Secretary of the Senate or Clerk of the House, respectively, before distribution. ➲

•

Committee Clerks

A clerk is assigned to each House and Senate committee to keep its records. These clerks report to the Chief Journal Clerk in the Senate and the Committee Clerk Supervisor in the House. These clerk supervisors have the following committee materials: a list of committees, committee assignments, committee postings, and roll calls. The House also provides audio recordings of committee hearings for a small fee. Copying fees may be charged for some committee records. ➲

•

Legislative Reference Bureau Publications

Illinois Bill Drafting Manual is published periodically (last updated January 2001). It describes in detail and illustrates the basic principles of drafting legislative documents.

Guide to Drafting Legislative Documents describes the legislative process and the associated documents, legal requirements, and provisions for drafting legislation, and provides illustrations of bill drafting techniques.

Researching Legislative History describes legislative documents and process and the methods of documenting legislative history.

Organization of the Illinois Compiled Statutes (ILCS) outlines the history and organizational principles of Illinois law.

Illinois Compiled Statutes (ILCS) and Alphabetical Index by Act is published annually. It lists the title of each state statute and includes an alphabetical index.

Illinois Compiled Statutes to Illinois Revised Statutes Cross-reference is an online publication.

•

Legislative Documents

Legislative Session Calendars are determined by the president of the Senate and speaker of the House at the beginning of, or just prior to, the spring session (January) and before the fall veto session (November). They are available in the Senate and House Bill Rooms, respectively, at other locations around the Statehouse, and online.

Daily Calendars are issued by the Senate and House each day the respective chamber is in session. The *Calendar* lists by number, name of chief sponsor, and topic all major business that may come before the chamber that day, including the time and place of any scheduled committee meetings. *Calendars* are available in the Senate and House Bill Rooms, respectively, in other locations around the Statehouse, and online.

Journals are issued two days to two weeks after each chamber meets by the Secretary of the Senate and Clerk of the House as a record of each chamber's activities on a given day. The *Journals* show all bills considered, the text of amendments considered, the roll calls of prior committee votes reported that day, and the results of all roll call votes taken on the chamber floor that day, among other things. *Journals* are available in the Senate and House Bill Rooms, respectively, and online.

Roll call votes that are recorded on bills, amendments, conference committee reports, and resolutions are available in the Journal Room of each chamber. When asking for a roll call vote record in a Journal Room, identify the bill number, the legislative action taken, and the date. Roll call votes are also recorded in the Senate and House *Journals* and online.

Access these documents online through the General Assembly Web site at http://www.legis.state.il.us/

•

Legislative Reporting and Tracking

These resources allow you to track legislation as it moves through the legislative process.

•

Legislative Information System (LIS)

Legislative Information System (LIS) is a legislative support agency that provides computer and technical support to the Illinois General Assembly. LIS provides the latest information on bill status, amendments, committee schedules, session times, and legislation. The LIS legislative tracking system was designed for use by legislators and their staff, but it is now available to the general public online. ➲

•

Senate Mail Room
Room 409 Statehouse
Telephone: (217) 782-9778

House Mail Room
O-Wing Stratton Building
Telephone: (217) 782-5238

Senate Chief Journal Clerk
Room 407 Statehouse
Telephone: (217) 782-2461

House Committee Clerk Supervisor
Room 115A Statehouse
Telephone: (217) 782-8100

Legislative Reference Bureau
Room112 Statehouse
Telephone: (217) 782-6625
http://www.legis.state.il.us/commission/lrb_home.html

Legislative Information System (LIS)
Room 705 Stratton Building
Telephone: (217) 782-3944
http://www.legis.state.il.us/commission/lis/lis_home.html

State Capital Information Service (SCIS)
300 East Monroe
Springfield, IL 62701
Telephone: (217) 523-6422
http://www.scisinc.com

Creative Resources
http://www.cr-illinois.com

LEGInfo.org
http://www.LEGInfo.org/

Illinois Compiled Statutes
Available in most public libraries and online at the General Assembly Web site at http://www.legis.state.il.us/. To purchase, contact the West Group at (312) 641-3075, or online at http://www.westgroup.com/

Illinois Administrative Code
For an annual subscription, call (217) 782-7017. To order part of the *Code*, call (217) 785-7538. For additional information, see http://www.library.sos.state.il.us/departments/index/divisions.html#admin_code. For the table of contents of the *Code*, see http://www.library.sos.state.il.us/departments/index/code/title.html

Legislative Reports

This is the most recent addition to the General Assembly Web site. These Reports can be extremely useful in tracking and monitoring legislation. The reports include: Bill Status Reports, Synopsis Reports, Categorized Reports, and Date Inquiry Reports.

•

State Capital Information Service (SCIS)

State Capital Information Service (SCIS) is the oldest privately run bill tracking and reporting system in the state. The bill tracking system is updated daily and allows as many user files and bills as the customer desires. Daily reports of all legislative actions are also available online or in hard copy for an annual fee. ℭ

•

Creative Resources of Illinois, Inc.

Creative Resources of Illinois provides an information service for tracking and monitoring legislation. Using the information provided by the LIS, Creative Resources provides Bill Introduction Reports, Adopted Amendment Reports, Status of Bills, Committee Information and Schedules, a Legislative Library, and links to other sources of information.

•

LEGInfo.org

This Web site was developed by the Center for Neighborhood Technology and sponsored by some not-for-profit groups to encourage citizen engagement in and knowledge of the legislative process. It provides legislative information on a variety of issues, including those related to children, education, the environment, health care, housing, land preservation, political reform, poverty, taxes and budgeting, transportation, and air quality. ℭ

Information on State Statutes

These resources allow you to document current state law in Illinois.

•

Public Acts

When a bill becomes law, the secretary of state assigns it a public act number. The number to the left of the hyphen indicates the number of the General Assembly that passed it, and the number to the right of the hyphen indicates the chronological order in which the legislation became law. For example, Public Act 91-0101 was the 101st bill signed into law during the 91st General Assembly. Copies of public acts are available upon request from the Secretary of State's Index Department or online at the General Assembly Web site.
Call (217) 782-7017, or see the General Assembly Web site at http://www.legis.state.il.us/

•

Laws of the State of Illinois

The secretary of state publishes this document annually, but it is only available in libraries. Also known as "Session Laws," this contains the complete text of all acts and joint resolutions signed into law during a legislative session, plus the governor's proclamations and executive orders.

•

Illinois Compiled Statutes (ILCS)

This document is published biennially by the Illinois State Bar Association in partnership with West Group. Formerly cited as the *Illinois Revised Statutes*, it integrates laws currently in effect in a codified, or subject, arrangement. The ILCS is available on the General Assembly Web site, which also includes a search capability. ℭ

•

Finding Administrative Rules and Regulations

These resources allow you to find administrative rules and monitor changes in them.

•

Illinois Administrative Code

Published by the secretary of state's office, the *Illinois Administrative Code* contains the adopted rules and regulations of all state agencies. The *Code* is available on CD-ROM for a fee, including the quarterly updates and indices. There is a copying fee to order only part of the *Code*. It is also available as a service of the Legislative Information Service and several private vendors, including Westlaw, Lexis-Nexus, and Law Office Information Services. ℭ

•

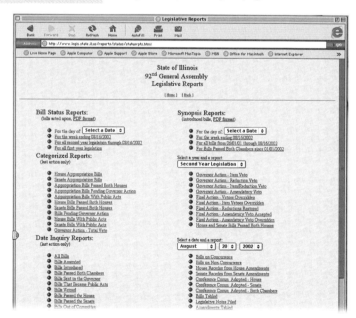

The Legislative Reports Web page provides a wealth of information about legislative activity in the General Assembly at http://www.legis.state.il.us/reports/status/statusrpts.html

Illinois Register

The *Illinois Register* is a weekly publication of the Secretary of State's Index Department announcing proposed, adopted, emergency, and other administrative rulemaking activities of all departments of state government. It is also available as a service of the Legislative Information Service and several private vendors, including Westlaw, Lexis-Nexus, and Law Office Information Services.

For an annual subscription, call (217) 782-0630. To access the table of contents for each *Illinois Register*, see http://www.library.sos.state.il.us/departments/index/register/register.html
For additional information, see http://www.library.sos.state.il.us/departments/index/divisions.html#admin_code

•

The Flinn Report: Illinois Regulation

Published weekly by the Joint Committee on Administrative Rules, this *Report* summarizes the rulemaking activity in each week's *Illinois Register*. The *Report* is an excellent tool for identifying issues you need to pursue more thoroughly in the *Illinois Register*. To subscribe, call (217) 785-2254, or see http://www.legis.state.il.us/commission/jcar/flinn_rpts.html

•

Information on the Governor

These are resources to obtain the governor's official public communications.

•

State of the State Address

The governor addresses the Illinois General Assembly at the beginning of its spring session and outlines the proposed plan of action for the State of Illinois for the next year. Public radio and television stations statewide carry the address live. Copies of the speech are available in print and online. ⊃

•

Budget Address

Each February, the governor addresses the General Assembly and outlines his or her proposed state budget for the next fiscal year. Public radio and television stations statewide carry the address live. Copies of the speech and the entire proposed budget are available in print and online. ⊃

•

Governor's Press Releases and Veto Messages

Obtain these documents from the appropriate member of the governor's staff. Press releases are available from the press secretary. Veto messages are available from the director of legislative affairs.
See the governor's Web site at: http://www.state.il.us/gov/govsteam/default.cfm

•

Information about State Finances

These resources document state government expenditures and revenues.

•

Fiscal Focus

Published by the state comptroller's office, this publication provides fiscal information of general interest to Illinois residents.
For a copy call (217) 782-6000, or see http://www.ioc.state.il.us/

•

Illinois State Budget

Each year, the governor proposes, and the General Assembly passes, the *Illinois State Budget*, which lays out in detail what state agencies are authorized to spend in a fiscal year. ⊃

•

The Economic and Fiscal Commission

As a support agency of the Illinois General Assembly, the Economic and Fiscal Commission keeps tabs on the state's economic and fiscal health and files a variety of reports with the Illinois General Assembly.
For more information call (217) 782-5320, or see http://www.legis.state.il.us/commission/ecfisc/ecfisc_home.html

•

Information on Elections

The Illinois State Board of Elections produces a number of publications and documents related to campaign finance, election results, and voter information. These include: *The Election Code of Illinois, Federal and State Officers, County Officers, Judicial*

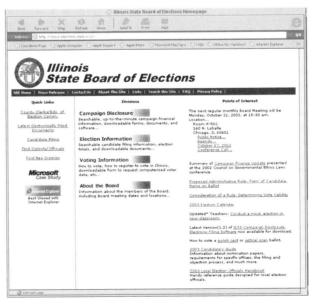

Illinois State Board of Elections Web site at http://www.elections.state.il.us.

Officers, Election and Campaign Finance Calendars, Candidate's Guide, Election Officials Handbook, and *Official Vote Totals.* The Board also supports an excellent database of campaign finance information searchable by candidate, committee, and contributor. For information call (217) 782-4141, or see http://www.elections.state.il.us/

•

Lobbyist Resources

These resources provide information about lobbyists working in Illinois.

•

Secretary of State's Index Department

The Index Department produces a variety of publications and information related to lobbyist registration and reporting including information on lobbying law, rules and regulations, registration and reporting forms, and a list of the registered lobbyists and entities in Illinois. Call (217) 782-0643, or see http://www.sos.state.il.us/departments/index/lobbyist_page.html

•

Current Affairs Publications and Media

Here are a variety of media resources that will allow you to keep current on policy and events in Illinois politics and government.

•

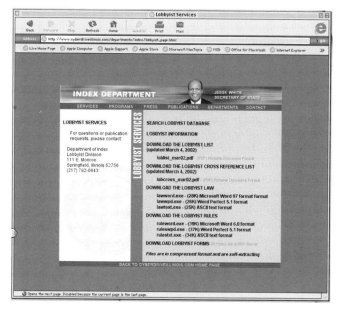

For Lobbyist Services, see the Secretary of State's Index Department's Web site at http://www.cyberdriveillinois.com/departments/index/lobbyist_page.html

Illinois Issues
Published monthly since 1975 by the University of Illinois at Springfield, this glossy magazine covers Illinois government and politics and other public issues of concern to Illinoisans. ↻

•

Capitol Fax
This two- to four-page newsletter is written and published by Rich Miller and faxed to subscribers daily during legislative sessions and less frequently at other times. Focused on political affairs and geared toward political insiders, it prints a subjective view of the current Statehouse grapevine. The associated Web site provides links to a wonderful array of governmental, legislative, and media Web sites. ↻

•

State Week in Review
This weekly radio show brings Statehouse reporters and commentators together to discuss the week's events in state politics and government. It is produced by WUIS-FM (in Springfield) and broadcast on most National Public Radio stations around the state. It can also be played anytime on the WUIS-FM Web site. ↻

•

First Reading
Published periodically by the Legislative Research Unit for state legislators, this newsletter provides a recap of end-of-session legislative activity and abstracts of legislative reports, along with other information. ↻

•

Illinois Politics
Published monthly by CNC publications, this publication focuses on Illinois state, Chicago, and Cook County government and politics. For information call (773) 283-7880, or see http://www.illinoispolitics.org/

•

Report on the Illinois Policy Survey
Published annually by the Center for Governmental Studies at Northern Illinois University in DeKalb, the *Report* summarizes the findings of the Illinois Policy Survey, which aims to assess the policy concerns of Illinoisans. For a copy call (815) 753-1918, or see http://www.cgsniu.org/pubs.htm#2000policy

•

UIS Politics and Policy Series
This is a series of public forums on political and policy issues in Illinois that are held at the University of Illinois at Springfield, broadcast on public radio and television, and available on videotape. For information on upcoming forums or to purchase videotapes, contact the Institute for Legislative Studies at (217) 206-6574, or see http://ils.uis.edu/

•

Information about Media Outlets

These resources provide information about the mass media and those who work in them in Illinois.

•

Illinois Media 2000

This publication contains a list of Illinois print and broadcast media, including broadcast and circulation areas, names of staff, and advertising rates. Call Midwest Newsclip at (312) 751-7300.

•

Illinois Press Association

The Illinois Press Association Web site provides a variety of information about the news media in the state. ⮕

•

Illinois Newspapers

Newspapers with significant coverage of Illinois state government include:
- *The State Journal-Register* (Springfield): http://www.sj-r.com/
- *Chicago Tribune*: http://www.chicagotribune.com/
- *Chicago Sun-Times*: http://www.suntimes.com/index/
- *St. Louis Post-Dispatch*: http://www.stlnet.com/
- *Daily Southtown* (Tinley Park): http://www.dailysouthtown.com/index/dsindex.html
- *The News-Gazette* (Champaign): http://www.news-gazette.com/

•

Statehouse Press Room

Located on the mezzanine between the second and third floors of the Statehouse, the Press Room includes the offices of the Statehouse press corps and press conference rooms. You can drop off press releases (approximately 40 copies) at the front desk for distribution to the press. Press conferences in the Statehouse must be scheduled with, but do not necessarily have to be held in, the Press Room. ⮕

•

Getting around the Statehouse and Capitol Complex

These resources will help you find your way around the Statehouse and Capitol Complex.

•

Secretary of State's Department of Physical Services

The Secretary of State's Department of Physical Services is responsible for the property management of the Capitol Complex, including maintenance, security, and special events. ⮕

•

Security

Visitors to the Capitol Complex are required to show photo identification and register at the door as they enter a building. To increase the efficiency of the operation, regular visitors to the Capitol Complex (such as legislators and lobbyists) may receive a special photo identification card from the Security Office, eliminating the need to register. ⮕

•

Illinois Press Association Web site
http://www.il-press.com/

Statehouse Press Room
West Mezzanine
Statehouse
Telephone: (217) 782-7664

Secretary of State's Department of Physical Services
Room 195
Howlett Building
Telephone: (217) 782-3896
For a map of the Capitol Complex, see http://www.sos.state.il.us/departments/physical_services/pscomplex.html

Statehouse Photo Identification Card
Security Office
Room 006 Howlett Bldg.
Telephone: (217) 782-3737.
Hours: 8:00a.m.-2:30p.m., Monday-Friday.

The Capitol Complex Visitors' Center at 425 South College Street, across from the Stratton Building.

Capitol Complex Visitors' Center

The Capitol Complex Visitors' Center is located at 425 South College Street, across from the Stratton Building. The Center provides information and a video presentation about the Capitol Complex. Limited parking is available, but the lot tends to fill up quickly when the legislature is in session.

Capitol Complex Visitors' Center
425 South College St.
Telephone: (217) 524-6620

•

Statehouse Information Desk

The Information Desk is in the rotunda on the first floor of the Statehouse. Guided tours of the building are offered daily from 8:00a.m. to 4:00p.m. except on Easter, Thanksgiving, Christmas, and New Year's Day. Reservations for group tours should be made in advance with the Springfield Convention and Visitors Bureau at (800) 545-7300. To contact the Statehouse Information Desk, call (217) 782-2099.

•

Welcome to the Illinois State Capitol

Published by the secretary of state, this brochure provides historical facts and figures on the construction of the Illinois Statehouse, including a diagram of the building. Copies are available at the Statehouse Information Desk. ℭ

•

Illinois State Capitol Sculptures: A Walking Tour

Produced by the secretary of state, this brochure provides a walking tour of the Capitol Complex, highlight-

ing the sculptures located around the grounds. It begins at the north entrance of the Statehouse and moves clockwise around the grounds. This brochure is available at the Capitol Complex Visitors' Center and the Statehouse Information Desk. To access this publication online, see http://www.sos.state.il.us/publications/stgovpub.html

•

The Illinois Statehouse Web Site

This Web site provides a history of the Statehouse, accompanied by a multitude of photos and illustrations. ℭ

•

Special Events in the Capitol Complex Facilities

If you want to hold a special event (such as a rally) at the Capitol Complex, you must obtain permission from the Secretary of State's Department of Physical Services' Special Events Division. ℭ

•

Room Reservations

The public hearing rooms in the Statehouse and the Stratton Building fall under the jurisdiction of the Secretary of the Senate and the Clerk of the House. These rooms may sometimes be used for meetings and events when the General Assembly is not in session and when the rooms are not otherwise occupied. For permission to use one of these rooms, contact the Secretary of the Senate for hearing rooms where Senate committees usually meet and the Clerk of the House for hearing rooms where House committees usually meet. ❏

The Statehouse Information Desk on the first floor of the rotunda.

Further Reading on Lobbying and Illinois Government

Banovetz, James M., ed. 1999. *Governing Illinois: Your Connection to State and Local Government*. Springfield, IL: Institute for Public Affairs.

Clements, John, ed. 1989. *Illinois Facts – Flying the Colors*. Dallas, TX: Clements Research II, Inc.

DeKieffer, Donald E. 1997. *The Citizen's Guide to Lobbying Congress*. Chicago: Chicago Review Press.

deVries, Christine, and Marjorie Vanderbilt. 1992. *The Grassroots Lobbying Handbook: Empowering Nurses through Legislative and Political Action*. Washington, DC: American Nurses Publishing.

Gove, Samuel K., and James D. Nowlan. 1996. *Illinois Politics and Government: The Expanding Metropolitan Frontier*. Lincoln, NE: University of Nebraska Press.

Gray, Virginia, and David Lowery. 1999. *The Population Ecology of Interest Representation: Lobbying Communities in the American States*. Ann Arbor, MI: University of Michigan Press.

Guyer, Robert L. 2000. *Guide to State Legislative Lobbying*. Gainesville, FL: Engineering the LAW, Inc.

Kenney, David, and Barb Brown. 1993. *Basic Illinois Government: A Systematic Explanation*. Carbondale, IL: Southern Illinois University Press.

Kleppner, Paul. 1988. *Political Atlas of Illinois*. DeKalb, IL: Northern Illinois University Press.

Kindell, Judith E., and John Francis Reilly. 1997. "Lobbying Issues." In *Exempt Organizations Continuing Professional Education Technical Instruction Program for FY 1997*. Washington, DC: Internal Revenue Service.

Mack, Charles. 1989. *Lobbying and Government Relations: A Guide for Executives*. Westport, CT: Quorum Books.

Meredith, Judith. 1989. *Lobbying on a Shoestring*. Westport, CT: Auburn House Publishing.

Nownes, Anthony J. 2001. *Pressure and Power: Organized Interests in American Politics*. Boston, MA: Houghton Mifflin.

Nownes, Anthony J., and Patricia Freeman. 1998. "Interest Group Activity in the American States." *Journal of Politics* 60:86-112.

Rosenthal, Alan. 1993. *The Third House: Lobbyists and Lobbying in the States*. Washington, DC: CQ Press.

Rosenthal, Alan. 1996. *Drawing the Line: Legislative Ethics in the States*. Lincoln, NE: University of Nebraska Press.

Rosenthal, Alan. 1998. *The Decline of Representative Democracy: Process, Participation, and Power in State Legislatures*. Washington, DC: CQ Press.

Rothenberg, Lawrence. 1992. *Linking Citizens to Government: Interest Group Politics at Common Cause*. New York: Cambridge University Press.

Smucker, Bob. 1999. *The Nonprofit Lobbying Guide*. 2nd ed. Washington, DC: Independent Sector.

Symms, Steven D., and Larry Grupp. 1994. *The Citizen's Guide to Fighting Government*. New York: Jameson Books.

Van Der Slik, Jack, and Kent Redfield. 1989. *Lawmaking in Illinois*. Springfield, IL: Institute for Public Affairs.

Wolpe, Bruce C., and Bertram J. Levine. 1996. *Lobbying Congress: How the System Works*. 2nd ed. Washington, DC: CQ Press.

Zorack, John L. 1990. *The Lobbying Handbook: A Comprehensive Lobbying Guide*. Washington, DC: Professional Lobbying and Consulting Center.

About the Authors

Christopher Z. Mooney is director of the Institute for Legislative Studies at the University of Illinois at Springfield. He has published five books and dozens of articles on state politics. He is also the editor of *State Politics and Policy Quarterly,* the leading political science journal in the field.

Barbara Van Dyke-Brown is assistant director of the Institute for Legislative Studies at the University of Illinois at Springfield. She has spent more than a decade working in and around the Illinois General Assembly. She is also the editor of the *Almanac of Illinois Politics - 2002*.